Junior Great Books®

Reader's Journal

Series 4   Book Two

This book belongs to:

The Great Books Foundation
A nonprofit educational organization

The interpretive discussion program that moves
students toward excellence in reading comprehension,
critical thinking, and writing

9 8 7 6
Printed in the United States of America

Cover art by Vivienne Flesher. Copyright © 2006 by Vivienne Flesher.
Text and cover design by William Seabright, William Seabright & Associates.
Interior design by Think Design Group.

Published and distributed by

The Great Books Foundation
A nonprofit educational organization
35 East Wacker Drive, Suite 400
Chicago, IL 60601

Welcome to Your Reader's Journal

This Reader's Journal is a place for you to collect your thoughts about the Junior Great Books stories you read and discuss in class. Here, you can be an artist and a poet, while discovering some secrets to becoming a strong reader and writer.

There are many parts of the Reader's Journal:

Writing Notebook allows you to gather some of your favorite pieces of writing in one place to revise and polish them.

Curious Words is where you can record the strange or interesting words you come across while reading. You don't have to memorize these words—you get to play with them, sounding them out in your head or out loud, or using them to make up messages and rhymes.

The **glossary** contains unusual or difficult words from the stories you've read. Look here for definitions that will help you better understand what you are reading.

Are you hunting for a **keeper question**, or do you have your **Head in the Clouds**? Maybe you're **Building Your Answer**, **Writing to Explain** or **Explore**, or getting **Into Reading**. Whatever you're working on, this Reader's Journal belongs to you. It's the place for your great ideas.

Contents

Shrewd Todie and Lyzer the Miser

Isaac Bashevis Singer

1

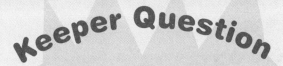
Keeper Question

In the space below, write a **keeper question** about the story that came into your mind during the first reading, while sharing questions, or even right now. Choose a question that no one has completely answered yet, and keep it in your mind during the second reading. If you still have the question after reading, continue to think about it—you picked a real keeper!

Your keeper question:

_____

_____

_____

_____

Into Reading
Making Inferences

Inferences can help you figure out things that are not directly stated in the story. To make an inference, you combine clues in the story with your own ideas.

- Read the passage and question below.

- Write your answer to the question.

- Circle word clues in the passage that helped you make an inference to answer the question.

Passage (page 12)

"Would you lend me . . . "
Even before Todie could finish the sentence, Lyzer interrupted. "You want to borrow a silver spoon? Take it with pleasure."

Question: How is Lyzer feeling about Todie's request to borrow a silver spoon again?

Your answer:

_____

_____

_____

_____

HEAD in the Clouds

Use your imagination! Choose one of the topics in the clouds and draw a picture or write a little more about the story.

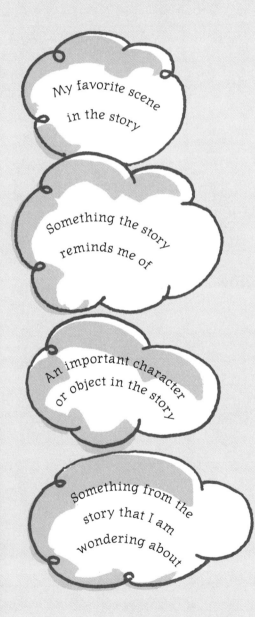

My favorite scene in the story

Something the story reminds me of

An important character or object in the story

Something from the story that I am wondering about

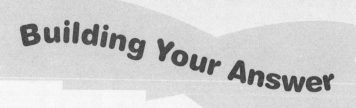

Building Your Answer

The focus question:

_____

_____

_____

_____

Your answer before the discussion:

_____

_____

_____

_____

Your answer after the discussion (you may change or add to your first answer):

_____

_____

_____

_____

_____

Writing to Explain
Writing About Character

Prewriting Notes

Complete the character web on the next page by filling in words that describe Todie. Add as many boxes as you want to the character web. Base your description on what is in the story.

Near each box, write one or two sentences about why you chose the word in the box. Use evidence from the story to support your answer.

> A **character** is someone in a story, play, or poem. **Character traits** tell what a character looks like, says, and does. They also tell how a character feels about people or things and how a character seems to other characters.

Writing to Explain
Writing About Character

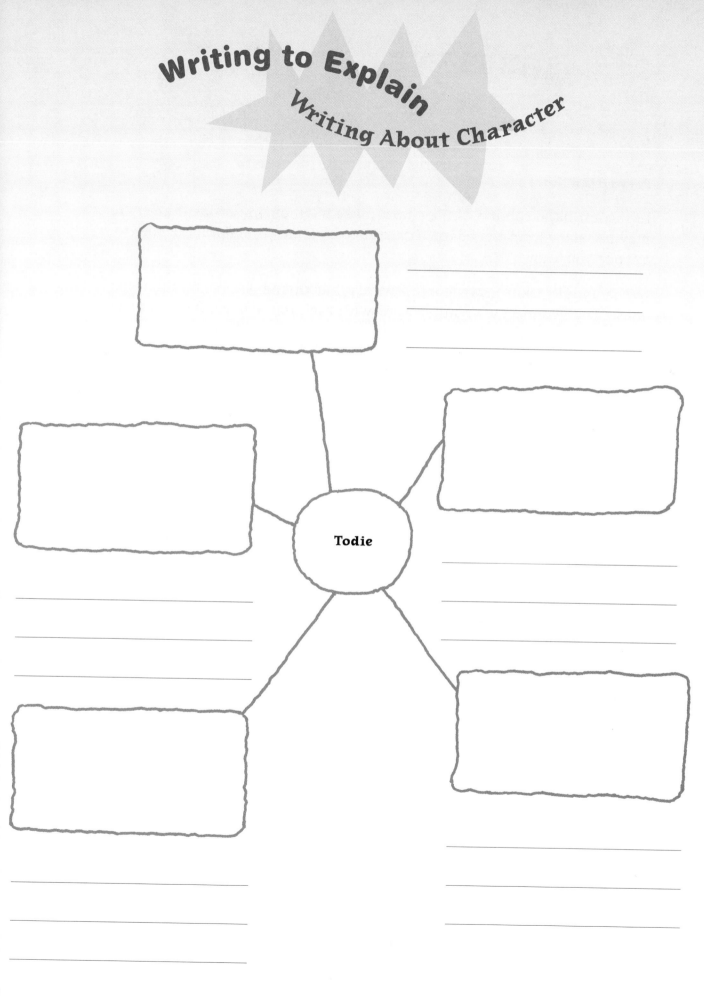

Todie

Writing to Explore
Nicknames

Prewriting Notes

In the left-hand column of the chart, make a list of first or last names. You may use some from the board. Try to choose names that do not belong to anyone you know.

In the middle column, write a few words that rhyme with each name you chose. Then connect a rhyming word with each name to create a nickname.

Name	Rhyming Words	Nickname

Circle your favorite nickname from the chart above. Write some details about a person who might have this nickname. Think about what this person looks or sounds like, where he or she lives, and what the person likes or dislikes.

Details:

Writing to Explore
Nicknames

Writing a Draft

Write a detailed description of your nicknamed person below. You may draw a picture of the person on the back of this page, if you wish.

_____

_____

_____

_____

_____

_____

_____

_____

_____

_____

_____

_____

_____

_____

_____

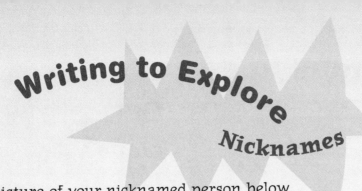

Writing to Explore
Nicknames

Draw a picture of your nicknamed person below.

The Goldfish

Eleanor Farjeon

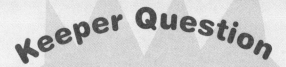

Keeper Question

In the space below, write a keeper question about the story that came into your mind during the first reading, while sharing questions, or even right now. Choose a question that no one has completely answered yet, and keep it in your mind during the second reading. If you still have the question after reading, continue to think about it—you picked a real keeper!

Your keeper question:

_____

_____

_____

_____

Into Reading

Making Inferences

Inferences can help figure out things that are not directly stated in the story. To make an inference, you combine clues in the story with your own ideas.

- Read the passage and question below.

- Write your answer to the question.

- Circle word clues in the passage that helped you make an inference to answer the question.

- Write down your own ideas that helped you make the inference.

Passage (pages 23–24)

"And you," said King Neptune, "have you never wept for these things?"

"Not I!" puffed the Porpoise. "What! Weep for the Sun and the Moon that are nothing but two blobs in the distance? Weep for the world that no one can behold? No, Father! When my dinner is in the distance, I'll weep for *that*; and when I see death coming, I'll weep for *that*; but for the rest, I say pooh!"

Continue ⟶

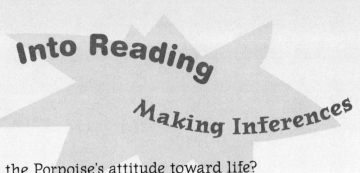

Into Reading

Making Inferences

Question: What is the Porpoise's attitude toward life?

Your answer:

_____

_____

_____

_____

Your own ideas that helped you make an inference to answer the question:

_____

_____

_____

_____

HEAD in the Clouds

Use your imagination! Choose one of the topics in the clouds and draw a picture or write a little more about the story.

A picture of a character in the story

Something I'm still wondering about

A sentence from the story that I liked, and why

My favorite moment in the story

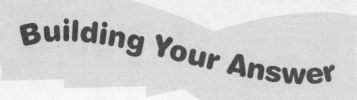

The focus question:

_____

_____

_____

Your answer before the discussion:

_____

_____

_____

Your answer after the discussion *(you may change or add to your first answer)*:

_____

_____

_____

_____

A part of the story that supports your answer:

_____

_____

_____

_____

Writing to Explain
Story Setting

Prewriting Notes

Complete the chart below by describing the two different settings in "The Goldfish." Then write down some of your ideas about why the change of setting in the story makes the Goldfish happier.

> The **setting** is the time and place of the story.

The sea	The fishbowl

Why do you think the change of setting makes the Goldfish happier?

_____

_____

_____

_____

Now use your notes to answer the question in an essay on the next page.

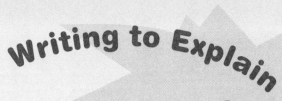

Writing to Explain
Story Setting

Writing a Draft

Answer this question in your essay: Why does a change of setting make the Goldfish happier?

Turn your prewriting notes into complete, detailed sentences. Use what you have learned about organizing an essay.

Writing to Explain
Story Setting

Use this page if you need more room.

_____

_____

_____

_____

_____

_____

_____

_____

_____

_____

_____

_____

_____

_____

_____

_____

_____

_____

Prewriting Notes

Write the name of one of your favorite places and some words or phrases to describe it. Think about what you hear, see, smell, taste, and touch when you visit this place to help you come up with details. Then write some **similes** about the details you wrote.

> A simile is a poetic comparison using the word **like** or **as**. A simile in "The Goldfish" is:
>
> "The great waves rose ╱ like ╲ mountains of glass" (page 19).

My Favorite Place: _____

Detail 1: _____

_____

Simile: _____

Detail 2: _____

_____

Simile: _____

Detail 3: _____

_____

Simile: _____

Writing to Explore
The Place to Be

Writing a Draft

Write a detailed description of your favorite place, using the similes that you wrote. Turn your notes into complete sentences and use as much detail as possible.

_____

_____

_____

_____

_____

_____

_____

_____

_____

_____

_____

_____

_____

Writing to Explore

The Place to Be

Use this page if you need more room.

_____

_____

_____

_____

_____

_____

_____

_____

_____

_____

_____

_____

_____

_____

_____

_____

_____

The Great Blackberry Pick

Philippa Pearce

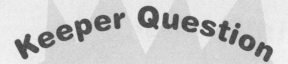

Keeper Question

In the space below, write a keeper question about the story that came into your mind during the first reading, while sharing questions, or even right now. Choose a question that no one has completely answered yet, and keep it in your mind during the second reading. If you still have the question after reading, continue to think about it—you picked a real keeper!

Your keeper question:

_____

_____

_____

_____

Inferences can help figure out things that are not directly stated in the story. To make an inference, you combine clues in the story with your own ideas.

- Read the passage and question below.

- Write your answer to the question.

- Circle word clues in the passage that helped you make an inference to answer the question.

- Write down your own ideas that helped you make the inference.

Passage (page 30)

—Chris said, "I'm not coming."

No one had ever said that to Dad before. What would happen? Dad began to growl in his throat like a dog preparing to attack. Then the rumble died away. Dad said, "Oh, have it your own way then."

Question: How is Dad feeling about Chris not going blackberry picking?

Your answer:

_____

_____

_____

_____

Your own ideas that helped you make the inference:

_____

_____

_____

_____

HEAD in the Clouds

Use your imagination! Choose one of the topics in the clouds and draw a picture or write a little more about the story.

The loneliest part of the story

Something the story reminds me of

A picture of a character in the story

A note to someone who has a bad temper

Building Your Answer

The focus question:

_____

_____

_____

Your answer before the discussion:

_____

_____

_____

_____

Your answer after the discussion (you may change or add to your first answer):

_____

_____

_____

_____

_____

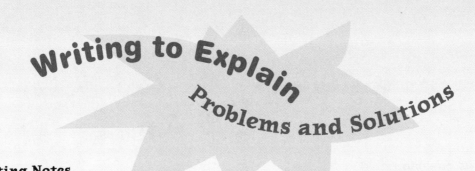

Writing to Explain
Problems and Solutions

Prewriting Notes

With a partner, write down Val's problems and solutions in the order they happen in the story.

A story **problem** happens when someone or something is working against a character.

A story **solution** happens when someone or something fixes the problem.

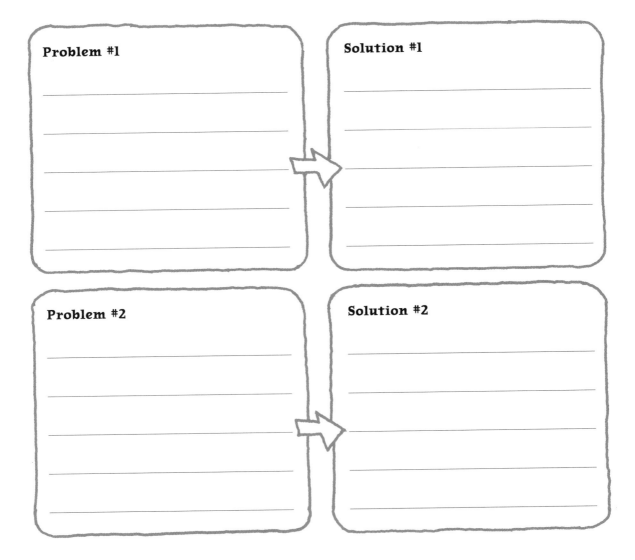

Problem #1

_____

_____

_____

_____

Solution #1

_____

_____

_____

_____

Problem #2

_____

_____

_____

Solution #2

_____

_____

_____

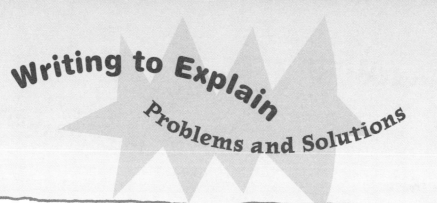

Writing to Explain
Problems and Solutions

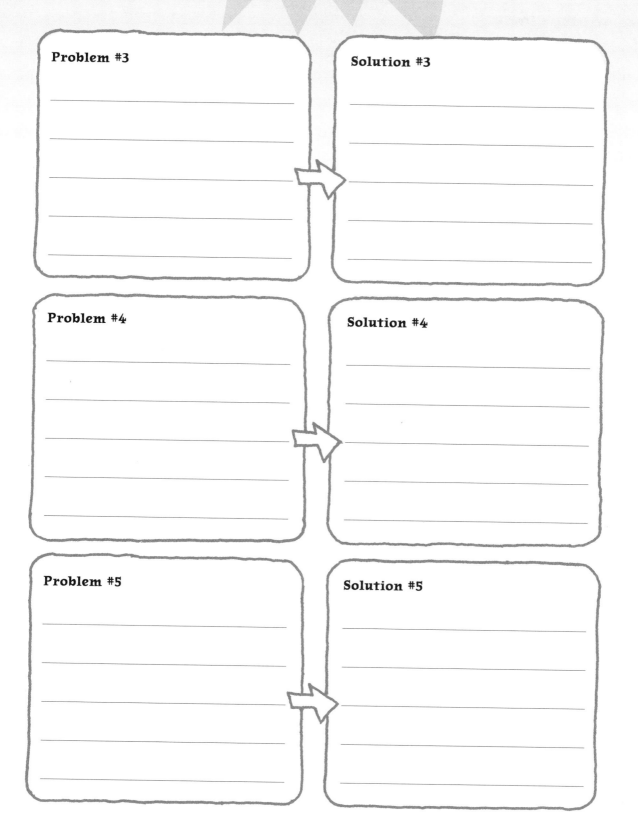

Problem #3

_____
_____
_____
_____
_____

Solution #3

_____
_____
_____
_____
_____

Problem #4

_____
_____
_____
_____
_____

Solution #4

_____
_____
_____
_____
_____

Problem #5

_____
_____
_____
_____
_____

Solution #5

_____
_____
_____
_____
_____

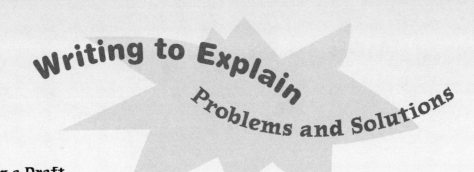

Writing a Draft

Look at the problems and solutions you wrote down. Think of another way Val could have solved one of her problems. Explain your answer in the space below.

_____

_____

_____

_____

_____

_____

_____

_____

_____

_____

_____

_____

_____

_____

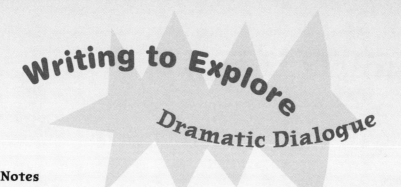

Writing to Explore
Dramatic Dialogue

Prewriting Notes

Write a few words, phrases, or quotes from the story that show both Val's and Dad's character traits (see page 6 of this Reader's Journal for more about character traits). This will help you think of things both characters might say to each other in a **dialogue**.

> **Dialogue** in a story is a conversation between two or more characters. Often, their words are set inside quotation marks.

Val's Character	Dad's Character
Example: Proud of being called pirate-girl (page 33)	Example: Stern (pages 31 and 32)

Writing to Explore
Dramatic Dialogue

Writing a Draft

Write a short dialogue between Val and Dad below, beginning right after they come home from looking for the red handkerchief. Use your notes to help you write dialogue that really sounds like Val and Dad are talking to each other.

Dad: "A day wasted!"

Val: _____

_____

_____

_____

_____

_____

_____

_____

_____

_____

_____

_____

The Story of Wang Li

Elizabeth Coatsworth

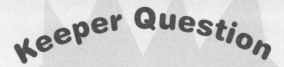

Keeper Question

In the space below, write down as your keeper question one of the interpretive questions you talked about in class. Then answer the question at the bottom of the page.

Your keeper question:

_____

_____

_____

_____

How did you decide to choose this question?

_____

_____

_____

_____

_____

_____

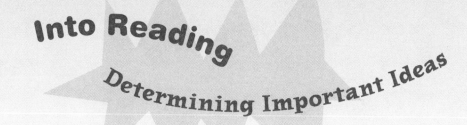

Into Reading

Determining Important Ideas

When you read, you decide which details are most important in helping you understand the story's main ideas or themes.

Read the following passage from the story.

Passage (page 54)

"If you would deign to take me away with you and allow me to serve your mother with my poor strength, I should no longer weep alone on this desolate mountain," she whispered.

"And what gifts would you bring my mother if I took you home as a bride?" asked Wang Li.

Then Precious Jade wrung her hands. "Alas," she said, "I have no gifts but only my will to serve you both." And she wept very bitterly.

At that Wang Li laughed and lifted her up in his arms and carried her home to his mother.

Continue ⟶

Into Reading
Determining Important Ideas

Write down some important words or phrases in the passage, what they mean in your own words, and the reason you think they are important. Look at the example if you need help.

Example

Some important words or details in this passage: "take me away with you" (page 54)

What these words or details mean (in your own words): Precious Jade wants to live on Wang Li's farm.

The reason you think these words or details are important: Precious Jade is different from the other women. She doesn't ask him to go where she lives.

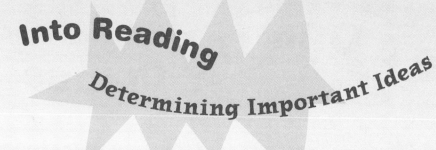

Into Reading
Determining Important Ideas

Some important words or details in this passage: _____

_____

_____

What these words or details mean (in your own words): _____

_____

_____

The reason you think these words or details are important: _____

_____

_____

Some important words or details in this passage: _____

_____

_____

What these words or details mean (in your own words): _____

_____

_____

The reason you think these words or details are important: _____

_____

HEAD in the Clouds

Use your imagination! Choose one of the topics in the clouds and draw a picture or write a little more about the story.

A place in the story that I would like to visit

Something in the story that I am curious about

A wish I would ask the Sky Damsel to grant me

Some reasons that I am like / not like Wang Li

Building Your Answer

The focus question:

_____

_____

_____

_____

Your answer before the discussion:

_____

_____

_____

_____

Your answer after the discussion (you may change or add to your first answer):

_____

_____

_____

_____

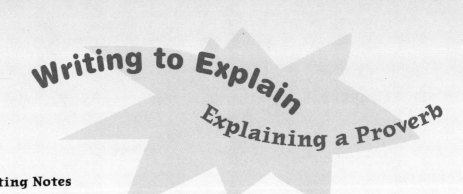

Writing to Explain
Explaining a Proverb

Prewriting Notes

Choose a proverb from "The Story of Wang Li" and explain it in the web below. If you need to, add more boxes to the web.

A **proverb** is a short saying that expresses a wise or common-sense idea in a creative way.

Proverb:

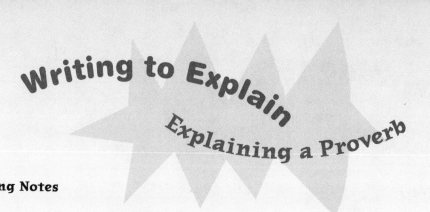

Writing to Explain
Explaining a Proverb

Prewriting Notes

Write some ideas in the space below about why Wang Li or his mother uses the proverb you chose. Carefully review the story for evidence to support your answer.

An event that happens just before the proverb:

_____

_____

_____

_____

_____

How that event is related to the proverb:

_____

_____

_____

_____

_____

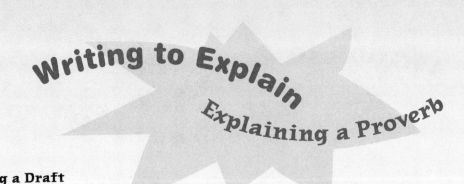

Writing to Explain

Explaining a Proverb

Writing a Draft

Look at your notes about the proverb you chose and answer this question in an essay: **Why does Wang Li or his mother quote the proverb you chose at that point in the story?** Give your essay a title that captures the reader's attention and has something to do with your main idea.

_____

_____

_____

_____

_____

_____

_____

_____

_____

_____

_____

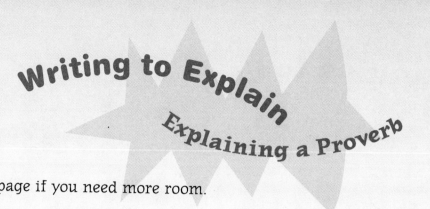

Writing to Explain
Explaining a Proverb

Use this page if you need more room.

_____

_____

_____

_____

_____

_____

_____

_____

_____

_____

_____

_____

_____

_____

_____

_____

_____

_____

Writing to Explore
A Letter to Little Splendor

Prewriting Notes

Imagine that you are Wang Li, writing a letter to Little Splendor after he has grown up. You will tell your son about one of the adventures you had before he was born. Choose an adventure from the story and write the **sequence of events** in the chart, along with details about each event. Then retell the events to a partner as though you are Wang Li. You can add more details based on your conversation with your partner.

Event 1: _____

_____

Details: _____

_____

Event 2: _____

_____

Details: _____

_____

Event 3: _____

_____

Details: _____

_____

_____

Event 4: _____

_____

Details: _____

_____

_____

Event 5: _____

_____

Details: _____

_____

_____

Writing to Explore
A Letter to Little Splendor

Writing a Draft

Using your prewriting notes, draft your letter to Little Splendor about an adventure you, Wang Li, once had. Include a salutation and a closing in your letter.

_____ ,

_____

_____

_____

_____

_____

_____

_____

_____

_____

_____ ,

Wang Li

The Hemulen Who Loved Silence

Tove Jansson

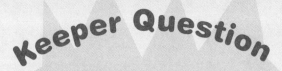

Keeper Question

In the space below, write down as your keeper question one of the interpretive questions you talked about in class. Then write down some parts of the story that relate to your keeper question in different ways.

Your keeper question:

_____

_____

_____

_____

Parts of the story that relate to your keeper question:

_____

_____

_____

_____

_____

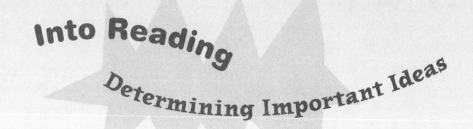
When you read, you decide which details are most important in helping you understand the story's main ideas or themes.

Read the following passage from the story.

Passage (pages 64–65)

"I'd like to build myself a doll's house," the hemulen whispered. "The most beautiful doll's house in the world, with lots and lots of rooms, and all of them silent and solemn and empty."

Now the hemulens laughed so hard that they had to sit down. They gave each other enormous nudges and shouted, "A doll's house! Did you hear that! He said a doll's house!" and then they laughed themselves into tears and told him:

"Little dear, by all means do exactly as you like! You can have grandma's big park, very probably it's silent as a grave nowadays."

Continue ⟶

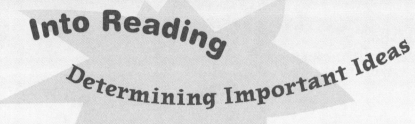

Into Reading
Determining Important Ideas

Write down some important words or phrases in the passage, what they mean in your own words, and the reason you think they are important. Look at the example if you need help.

Example

Some important words or details in this passage: " 'I'd like to build myself a doll's house,' the hemulen whispered." (page 64)

What these words or details mean (in your own words)**:** The hemulen shyly tells others his dream.

The reason you think these words or details are important:
Although he might be nervous about it, the hemulen is finally saying what he wants.

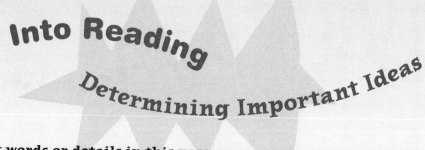

Some important words or details in this passage: _____

_____

_____

What these words or details mean (in your own words): _____

_____

_____

The reason you think these words or details are important: _____

_____

_____

Some important words or details in this passage: _____

_____

_____

What these words or details mean (in your own words): _____

_____

_____

The reason you think these words or details are important: _____

_____

_____

HEAD in the Clouds

Use your imagination! Choose one of the topics in the clouds and draw a picture or write a little more about the story.

A picture of the pleasure ground or old park

A picture of the hemulen doing something he likes

A note to the hemulen

A sentence from the story that I liked, and why

Building Your Answer

The focus question:

_____

_____

_____

Your answer before the discussion:

_____

_____

_____

Your answer after the discussion (_you may add to or change your first answer_):

_____

_____

_____

Two pieces of evidence from the story that support your answer:

1. _____

   _____

   _____

2. _____

   _____

   _____

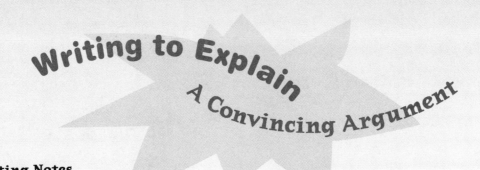

Writing to Explain
A Convincing Argument

Prewriting Notes

Below, write three reasons the characters in the story might like visiting the pleasure ground. Then, write three reasons other characters (such as the whomper, the kiddies, or the other hemulens) might like visiting the Park of Silence. Base your reasons on what the characters say or do in the story.

Reasons to visit the pleasure ground:

1. _____

_____

2. _____

_____

3. _____

_____

Reasons to visit the Park of Silence:

1. _____

_____

2. _____

_____

3. _____

_____

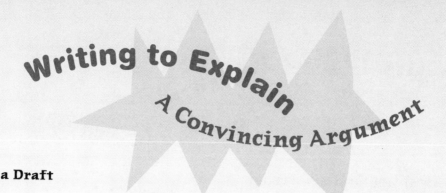

Writing to Explain
A Convincing Argument

Writing a Draft

Write an essay to convince the story characters to visit the Park of Silence. Using your prewriting notes, offer some reasons that it might be nice to visit the pleasure ground, and then explain why visiting the Park of Silence would be a better choice. Give your essay a title that captures the reader's attention and has something to do with your main idea.

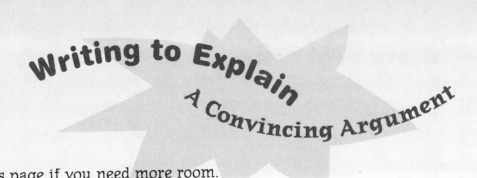

Writing to Explain
A Convincing Argument

Use this page if you need more room.

_____

_____

_____

_____

_____

_____

_____

_____

_____

_____

_____

_____

_____

_____

_____

_____

_____

_____

_____

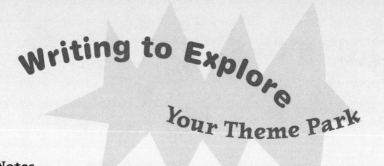

Writing to Explore
Your Theme Park

Prewriting Notes

Imagine that you can build a theme park that shows your interests and personality, just like the hemulen's Park of Silence. What kind of park would you build? Write the name of your park in the middle box of the web on the next page.

Choose four topics related to theme parks, such as "Food and Drink" or "Rides and Games," and add details about your park underneath the topics you selected.

After You've Completed the Web

Remember that the hemulen built his Park of Silence because he wanted to be in a quiet place by himself. Why would you build your park? Who else might want to visit it? Why?

_____

_____

_____

_____

_____

_____

Continue ⟶

Writing to Explore Your Theme Park

Topic 1:

Details: _____

_____

_____

_____

_____

Topic 2:

Details: _____

_____

_____

_____

_____

My Theme Park:

_____

Topic 3:

Details: _____

_____

_____

_____

_____

Topic 4:

Details: _____

_____

_____

_____

_____

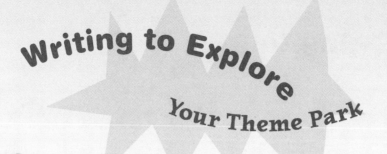

Writing to Explore Your Theme Park

Writing a Draft

Use your prewriting notes to write a detailed description of your theme park. End your description by explaining why you would build your park and who else might enjoy visiting it (and why). Give your description a title that captures the reader's attention.

_____

_____

_____

_____

_____

_____

_____

_____

_____

_____

_____

_____

_____

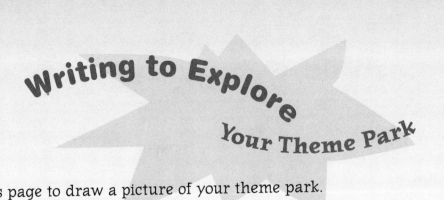

Writing to Explore
Your Theme Park

Use this page to draw a picture of your theme park.

The Enchanted Sticks

Steven J. Myers

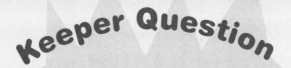

Keeper Question

In the space below, write down as your keeper question one of the interpretive questions you talked about in class. Then write down two parts of the story that relate to your keeper question.

Your keeper question:

_____

_____

_____

_____

Two parts of the story that relate to your keeper question:

1. _____

_____

_____

_____

2. _____

_____

_____

_____

Into Reading
Determining Important Ideas

When you read, you decide which details are most important in helping you understand the story's main ideas or themes.

- Find a passage in the story you marked with an **!** and reread it.
  Write an important phrase or sentence from that part of the story.

- Write what you think that phrase or sentence means.

- Write your reasons for thinking this phrase or sentence is important.

1. An important phrase or sentence from the story:

_____

_____ (page _____)

What this phrase or sentence means (in your own words):

_____

_____

The reason you think this phrase or sentence is important:

_____

_____

_____

Continue ⟶

2. An important phrase or sentence from the story:

_____

_____ (page _____)

What this phrase or sentence means (in your own words):

_____

_____

The reason you think this phrase or sentence is important:

_____

_____

_____

3. An important phrase or sentence from the story:

_____

_____ (page _____)

What this phrase or sentence means (in your own words):

_____

_____

The reason you think this phrase or sentence is important:

_____

_____

_____

HEAD in the Clouds

Use your imagination! Choose one of the topics in the clouds and draw a picture or write a little more about the story.

The most magical part of the story

A picture of the enchanted sticks writing a message

A conversation I would have with one of the characters

Something that I'm still wondering about

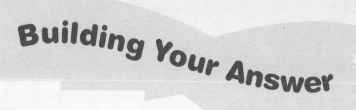

The focus question:

_____

_____

_____

Your answer before the discussion:

_____

_____

_____

Your answer after the discussion (you may change or add to your first answer):

_____

_____

_____

_____

An answer you heard in the discussion that was different from yours:

_____

_____

_____

_____

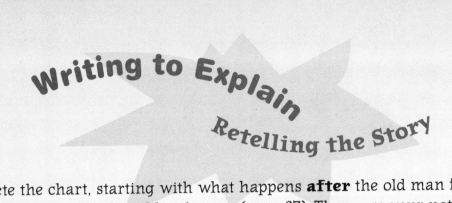

Writing to Explain
Retelling the Story

Complete the chart, starting with what happens **after** the old man follows the maiden's song to the robbers' camp (page 87). Then, use your notes to retell that part of the story to a partner in your own words.

> The **sequence of events** is the order in which things happen in the story.

Event

1. _____

_____

2. _____

_____

3. _____

_____

4. _____

_____

5. _____

_____

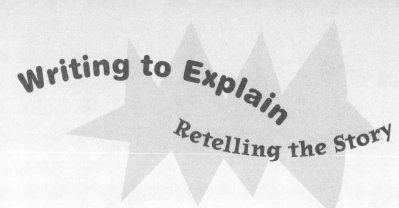

Writing to Explain
Retelling the Story

Setting	Characters' responses
1. _____ _____	1. _____ _____
2. _____ _____	2. _____ _____
3. _____ _____	3. _____ _____
4. _____ _____	4. _____ _____
5. _____ _____	5. _____ _____

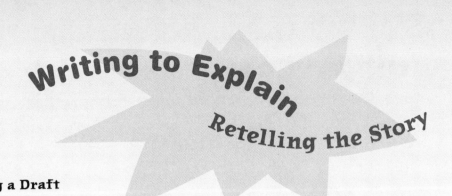

Writing to Explain
Retelling the Story

Writing a Draft

Using your own words, describe what happens in "The Enchanted Sticks" after the old man follows the maiden's song to the robbers' camp. Put the story events in the correct order, using your prewriting notes to help you.

From "The Enchanted Sticks": Your Own Words

After the old man follows the maiden's song to the robbers' camp,

_____

_____

_____

_____

_____

_____

_____

_____

_____

_____

_____

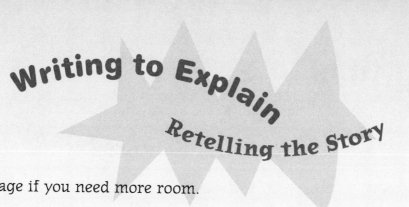

Writing to Explain
Retelling the Story

Use this page if you need more room.

_____

_____

_____

_____

_____

_____

_____

_____

_____

_____

_____

_____

_____

_____

_____

_____

_____

_____

Writing to Explore
An Enchanted Object

Prewriting Notes

With your partner, choose an object that you would like to write about.
If the object were enchanted, think of how it could help you solve a problem.
You can make up a problem, or write about a problem that you really have.

Your partner's name: _____

Your object: _____

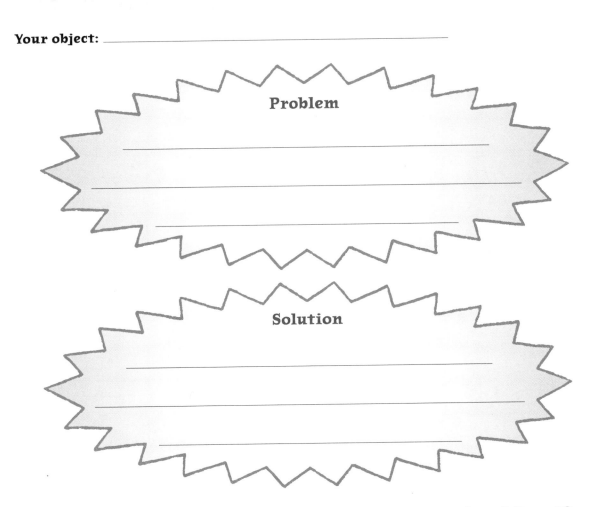

Problem

Solution

Once your problem is solved, what would you do with your object? Keep it?
Give it away? Turn it into something else? Write your answer below.

_____

_____

_____

Writing to Explore
An Enchanted Object

Writing a Draft

Using your notes, draft your story in the space below. It should end with you and your partner deciding what to do with your object. Remember to turn your prewriting notes into complete, detailed sentences and to give your story an interesting title.

Writing to Explore
An Enchanted Object

Use this page if you need more room.

_____

_____

_____

_____

_____

_____

_____

_____

_____

_____

_____

_____

_____

_____

_____

_____

_____

_____

_____

_____

The Elephant's Child

Rudyard Kipling

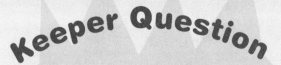

Keeper Question

In the space below, write down an interpretive question. Then write down two possible answers and a part of the story that supports each answer.

Your keeper question:

_____

_____

_____

_____

One way to answer the question: _____

_____

_____

A part of the story that supports this answer: ____

_____

_____

Another way to answer the question: _____

_____

_____

A part of the story that supports this answer: ____

_____

_____

Into Reading

Synthesizing

Synthesizing means you are thinking about different parts of a story and putting your thoughts together in a way that helps you understand the story's main ideas or themes. Synthesizing is like putting the pieces of a puzzle together to create a whole picture. When you synthesize, you use many other reading strategies, too.

In the box below, list in order three important events that happen after the Elephant's Child spends three days waiting for his nose to shrink (page 100 of the story).

Important events (in order)

1. _____

_____

_____

2. _____

_____

_____

3. _____

_____

_____

Continue ⟶

Synthesizing

Look at the important events you listed on page 79. In the box below, write a summary about that part of the story.

Remember that a good **summary** includes enough information to explain what this part of the story is about, but not so much detail that you are just retelling the story step by step. Your summary should be one to two sentences long.

Summary

Now, in the box below, write some of your own thoughts about the story. You can write a question, a connection, an inference, your opinion, or anything else.

Your response

HEAD in the Clouds

Use your imagination! Choose one of the topics in the clouds and draw a picture or write a little more about the story.

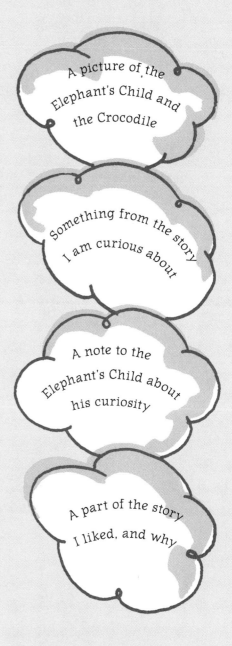

A picture of the Elephant's Child and the Crocodile

Something from the story I am curious about

A note to the Elephant's Child about his curiosity

A part of the story I liked, and why

Building Your Answer

The focus question:

_____

_____

_____

_____

Your answer before the discussion:

_____

_____

_____

_____

Your answer after the discussion _(you may change or add to your first answer)_:

_____

_____

_____

_____

_____

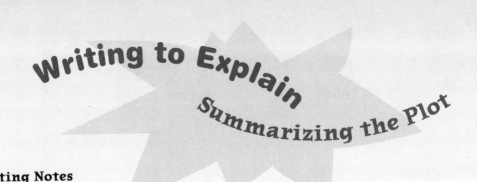

Writing to Explain
Summarizing the Plot

Prewriting Notes

Complete the plot chart below.

> A story's **plot** is the sequence of events that occurs in the story. The plot also includes the setting and the characters' responses to the events.

Event

1. _____

   _____

2. _____

   _____

3. _____

   _____

4. _____

   _____

5. _____

   _____

Writing to Explain
Summarizing the Plot

Setting	Characters' responses
1. _____ _____	1. _____ _____
2. _____ _____	2. _____ _____
3. _____ _____	3. _____ _____
4. _____ _____	4. _____ _____
5. _____ _____	5. _____ _____

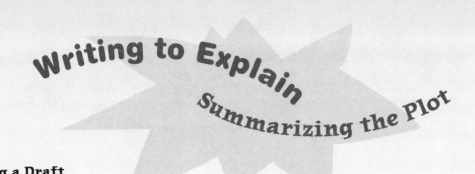

Writing to Explain
Summarizing the Plot

Writing a Draft

Write a summary of "The Elephant's Child." Use your plot chart to help you remember important events in the story.

Remember that a **summary** should include enough information to explain what the story is about, but not so much detail that you are retelling the entire story step by step.

A Summary of "The Elephant's Child"

_____

_____

_____

_____

_____

_____

_____

_____

_____

_____

_____

_____

_____

_____

Writing to Explain
Summarizing the Plot

Use this page if you need more room.

_____

_____

_____

_____

_____

_____

_____

_____

_____

_____

_____

_____

_____

_____

_____

_____

Prewriting Notes

In "The Elephant's Child," Rudyard Kipling uses **portmanteau words** (made-up words that combine two real ones) to describe things in an interesting, original way. For example, "curtiosity" can be seen as a combination of "curious" and "courteous."

Choose an animal you would like to describe using portmanteau words. Think about this animal and write some of the words or phrases that come into your mind in the web below.

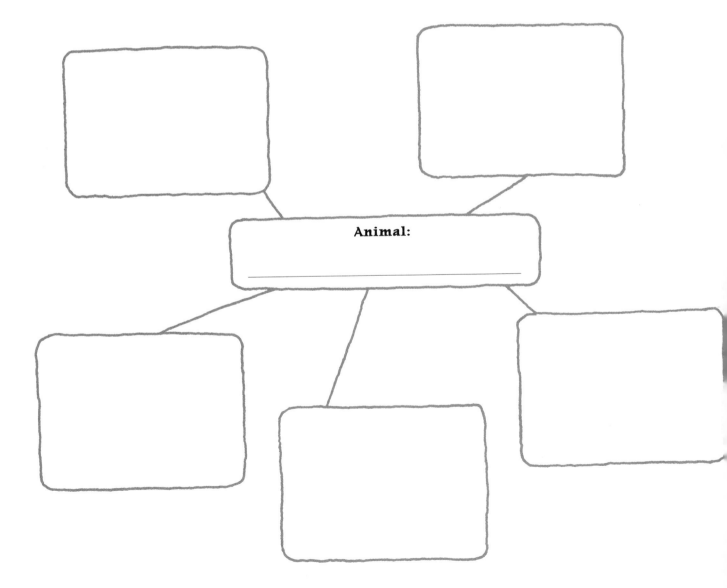

Animal: _____

Writing to Explore
Splendiferous 'Scriptions

Prewriting Notes

Here are some examples of **portmanteau words** created to describe a parrot:

- feathers + imitating = **featherating**

- flapping + squawking = **flawking**

- yellow + loud = **yelloud**

Now use the words in your web to create portmanteau words to describe your animal. Write them below.

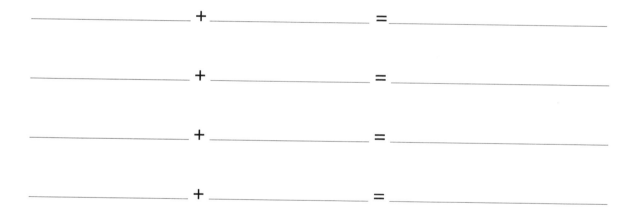

Writing to Explore
Splendiferous 'Scriptions

Writing a Draft

Write a paragraph describing a day in the life of your animal, using the portmanteau words you created. Remember to turn your notes into complete sentences. Give your description an interesting title.

_____

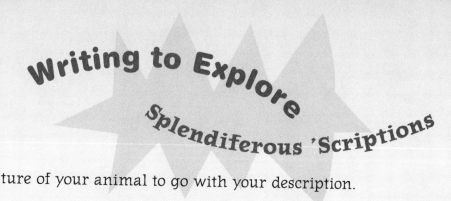

Writing to Explore
Splendiferous 'Scriptions

Draw a picture of your animal to go with your description.

Mr. Singer's Nicknames

James Krüss

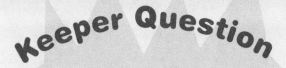

Keeper Question

In the space below, write down an interpretive question. Then write down two possible answers and a part of the story that supports each answer.

Your keeper question: _____

_____

_____

_____

_____

One way to answer the question: _____

_____

_____

A part of the story that supports this answer: _____

_____

_____

Another way to answer the question: _____

_____

_____

A part of the story that supports this answer: _____

_____

_____

Into Reading

Synthesizing

Synthesizing means you are thinking about different parts of a story and putting your thoughts together in a way that helps you understand the story's main ideas or themes. Synthesizing is like putting the pieces of a puzzle together to create a whole picture. When you synthesize, you use many different reading strategies.

In the box below, list in order three important events that happen after Mr. Singer loses the bet and climbs into the rowboat with the pastor (page 116 of the story).

Important events (in order)

1. _____

_____

_____

_____

2. _____

_____

_____

_____

3. _____

_____

_____

_____

Continue ⟶

Into Reading

Synthesizing

Look at the important events you listed on the previous page. In the box below, write a summary of that part of the story below.

> Remember that a good **summary** includes enough information to explain what this part of the story is about, but not so much detail that you are just retelling the story step by step. Your summary should be one to two sentences long.

Summary

_____

_____

_____

_____

Now, in the box below, write some of your own thoughts about the story. You can write a question, a connection, an inference, your opinion, or anything else.

Your response

_____

_____

_____

_____

HEAD in the Clouds

Use your imagination! Choose one of the topics in the clouds and draw a picture or write a little more about the story.

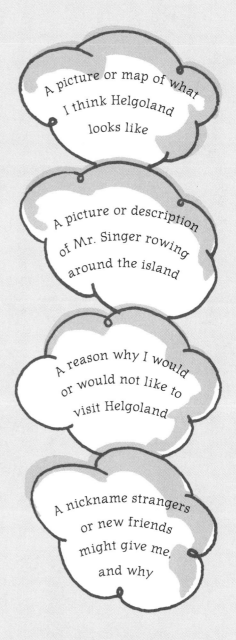

A picture or map of what I think Helgoland looks like

A picture or description of Mr. Singer rowing around the island

A reason why I would or would not like to visit Helgoland

A nickname strangers or new friends might give me, and why

Building Your Answer

The focus question:

_____

_____

_____

Your answer before the discussion:

_____

_____

_____

Your answer after the discussion (you may change or add to your first answer):

_____

_____

_____

Two quotes or brief passages from the story that support your answer:

1. _____

_____

_____

2. _____

_____

_____

Writing to Explain
Writing About Theme

Prewriting Notes

Choose a theme in "Mr. Singer's Nicknames." Then complete the web below by filling in evidence from the story that supports that theme.

A **theme** is a major idea in a story. A theme goes beyond the characters and events in the story. It has to do with the story's overall meaning or with something important the author is trying to say.

Theme:

_____

_____

_____

_____

Writing to Explain
Writing About Theme

Evidence: (page _____)

_____

_____

_____

_____

_____

Evidence: (page _____)

_____

_____

_____

_____

_____

Evidence: (page _____)

_____

_____

_____

_____

_____

Writing to Explain
Writing About Theme

Writing a Draft

Write an essay explaining the theme you chose and giving evidence from the story that tells the reader about that theme.

_____

_____

_____

_____

_____

_____

_____

_____

_____

_____

_____

_____

_____

_____

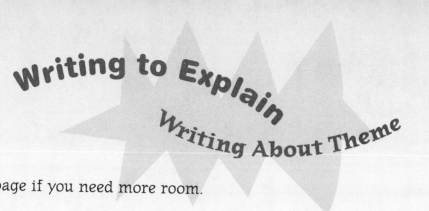

Writing to Explain

Writing About Theme

Use this page if you need more room.

_____

_____

_____

_____

_____

_____

_____

_____

_____

_____

_____

_____

_____

_____

_____

_____

_____

_____

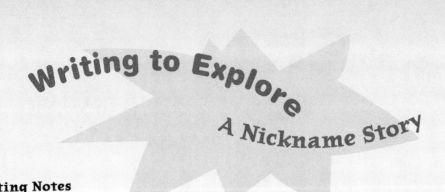

Writing to Explore
A Nickname Story

Prewriting Notes

Write a nickname of a character you want to write a story about. Then complete the chart. Your story should include details about what the person used to be like before he or she got a nickname; the change or problem that caused that person to get a nickname, and what the person is like now.

Character's Nickname: _____

> Your story's **beginning** (how the person used to be)
>
> Example: Shirley was always late for school.
>
> _____
>
> _____
>
> _____
>
> _____
>
> _____

Writing to Explore
A Nickname Story

Your story's **middle** (an event, problem, or change that leads to the nickname)

Example: One day, she found magic shoes that made her run faster than the wind.

_____

_____

_____

_____

_____

Your story's **end** (how the person is now because of what happened)

Example: Now she gets to school before it even opens. So we call her **Early Shirley.**

_____

_____

_____

_____

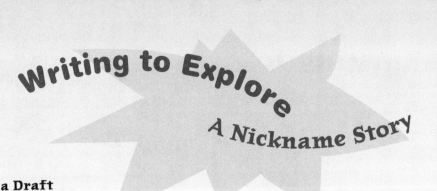

Writing to Explore
A Nickname Story

Writing a Draft

Using your notes, draft a story about how your character got his or her nickname. Remember that your story should have a beginning, a middle, and an end. Give your story an interesting title.

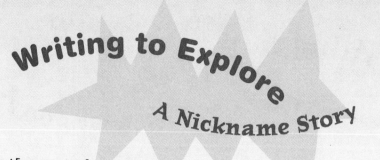

Writing to Explore
A Nickname Story

Use this page if you need more room.

_____

_____

_____

_____

_____

_____

_____

_____

_____

_____

_____

_____

_____

_____

_____

_____

_____

Writing to Explore

A Nickname Story

Use this page to draw a picture of your character or a scene from your story.

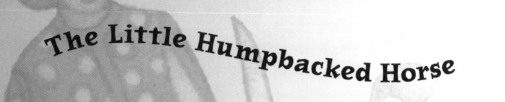

The Little Humpbacked Horse

Russian folktale as told by Post Wheeler

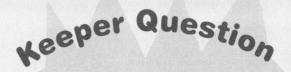

Keeper Question

In the space below, write down an interpretive question. Then write down two possible answers and a passage from the story that supports each answer.

Your keeper question:

_____

_____

_____

One way to answer the question: _____

_____

_____

A passage that supports this answer: _____

_____

_____ (page _____)

Another way to answer the question: _____

_____

_____

A passage that supports this answer: _____

_____

_____ (page _____)

Into Reading

Synthesizing

Synthesizing means you are thinking about different parts of a story and putting your thoughts together in a way that helps you understand the story's main ideas or themes. Synthesizing is like putting the pieces of a puzzle together to create a whole picture. When you synthesize, you use many different reading strategies.

Choose a part of the story you think is important or interesting. In the box below, list in order three important events that happen in this part of the story.

The part of the story I chose is on page _____ .

Important events (in order)

1. _____
   _____
   _____

2. _____
   _____
   _____

3. _____
   _____
   _____

Continue ⟶

Into Reading

Synthesizing

Look at the important events you listed on the previous page. Write a summary of that part of the story below.

Remember that a good **summary** includes enough information to explain what this part of the story is about, but not so much detail that you are just retelling the story step by step. Your summary should be one or two sentences long.

Your summary:

_____

_____

_____

_____

Write some of your own thoughts about what happened in the story. You can write a question, a connection, an inference, your opinion, or anything else.

Your thoughts:

_____

_____

_____

_____

HEAD in the Clouds

Use your imagination! Choose one of the topics in the clouds and draw a picture or write a little more about the story.

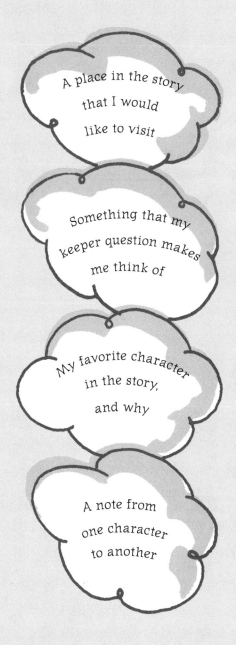

A place in the story that I would like to visit

Something that my keeper question makes me think of

My favorite character in the story, and why

A note from one character to another

Building Your Answer

The focus question:

_____

_____

_____

Your answer before the discussion:

_____

_____

_____

_____

Your answer after the discussion (you may change or add to your first answer):

_____

_____

_____

_____

An answer you heard in discussion that is different from yours:

_____

_____

_____

_____

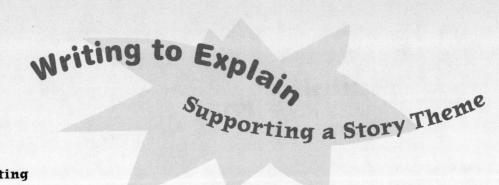

Writing to Explain
Supporting a Story Theme

Prewriting

Choose a theme in "The Little Humpbacked Horse" and take some notes on how each piece of evidence you choose supports your theme.

Theme:

_____

_____

_____

_____

Writing to Explain
Supporting a Story Theme

Evidence: (page _____)

Explanation:

_____

_____

_____

_____

_____

_____

_____

_____

_____

Evidence: (page _____)

Explanation:

_____

_____

_____

_____

_____

_____

_____

_____

_____

Evidence: (page _____)

Explanation:

_____

_____

_____

_____

_____

_____

_____

_____

_____

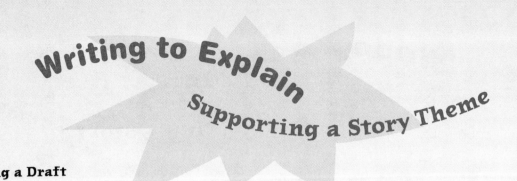

Writing to Explain
Supporting a Story Theme

Writing a Draft

Using your notes, write an essay that explains your chosen theme for "The Little Humpbacked Horse." Remember to choose and explain your evidence from the story.

_____

_____

_____

_____

_____

_____

_____

_____

_____

_____

_____

_____

_____

_____

_____

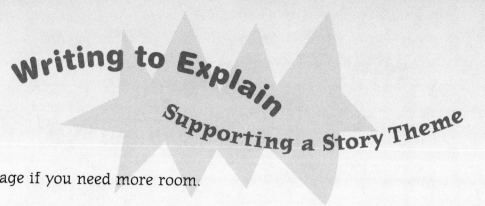

Writing to Explain
Supporting a Story Theme

Use this page if you need more room.

_____

_____

_____

_____

_____

_____

_____

_____

_____

_____

_____

_____

_____

_____

_____

_____

_____

_____

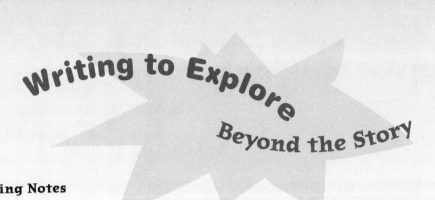

Writing to Explore
Beyond the Story

Prewriting Notes

In "The Little Humpbacked Horse," Ivan lets the white mare go after she bears three colts. Use your imagination to write in the chart below about what happens to the mare after Ivan lets her go.

Event
1.
2.
3.
4.
5.

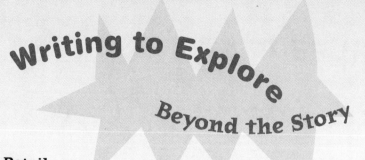

Writing to Explore
Beyond the Story

Describing in Detail

As you think of more details, ask:

• Where is the white mare now? What does it look like there?

• What are some of the things she sees/hears/smells/tastes/touches?

• Does she meet any more characters? What are they like?

Setting	Characters' responses
1. _____ _____	1. _____ _____
2. _____ _____	2. _____ _____
3. _____ _____	3. _____ _____
4. _____ _____	4. _____ _____
5. _____ _____	5. _____ _____

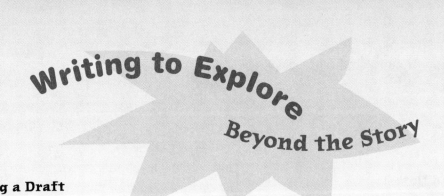

Writing to Explore
Beyond the Story

Writing a Draft

Using your sequencing chart, write your story about what happens to the mare after Ivan lets her go. Include as much detail about each event as possible. Remember to give your essay an interesting title.

_____

_____

_____

_____

_____

_____

_____

_____

_____

_____

_____

_____

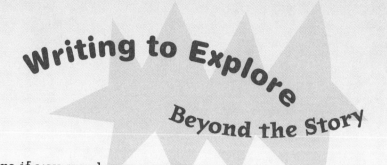

Writing to Explore

Beyond the Story

Use this page if you need more room.

_____

_____

_____

_____

_____

_____

_____

_____

_____

_____

_____

_____

_____

_____

_____

_____

_____

_____

_____

Ali Baba and the Forty Thieves

from _The Arabian Nights_

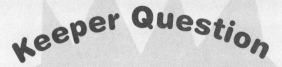

Keeper Question

In the space below, write down an interpretive question. Then write down two possible answers and a passage from the story that supports each answer.

Your keeper question:

_____

_____

_____

One way to answer the question: _____

_____

_____

A passage that supports this answer: _____

_____

_____ (page _____)

Another way to answer the question: _____

_____

_____

A passage that supports this answer: _____

_____

_____ (page _____)

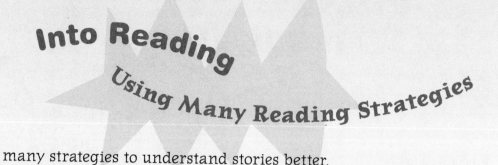

Into Reading
Using Many Reading Strategies

Readers use many strategies to understand stories better.

- Choose two passages you marked with check marks (✓). (The check marks show that you wanted to remember your thoughts about the story.)

- Write about what you were thinking when you marked each passage.

- Write the strategy you used, choosing from this list:
  - Asking questions
  - Making connections
  - Visualizing
  - Making inferences
  - Determining important ideas

Passage 1 (page _____)

_____

_____

_____

What you were thinking about when you marked the passage:

_____

_____

_____

The reading strategy you used (you may have used more than one):

_____

_____

Continue ⟶

Ali Baba and the Forty Thieves Page 127

Passage 2 (page _____)

_____

_____

_____

_____

What you were thinking about when you marked the passage:

_____

_____

_____

_____

The reading strategy you used *(you may have used more than one)*:

_____

_____

HEAD in the Clouds

Use your imagination! Choose one of the topics in the clouds and draw a picture or write a little more about the story.

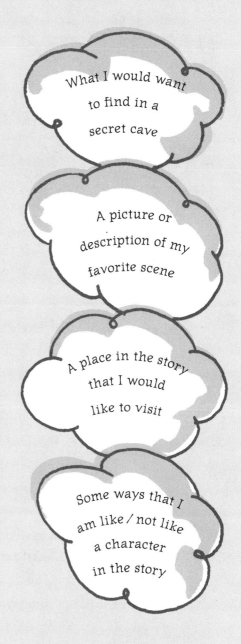

What I would want to find in a secret cave

A picture or description of my favorite scene

A place in the story that I would like to visit

Some ways that I am like / not like a character in the story

Building Your Answer

The focus question:

_____

_____

_____

Your answer before the discussion:

_____

_____

_____

_____

Your answer after the discussion (you may change or add to your first answer):

_____

_____

_____

_____

To support your answer, write one piece of evidence from the story _or_ something you heard in the discussion:

_____

_____

_____

_____

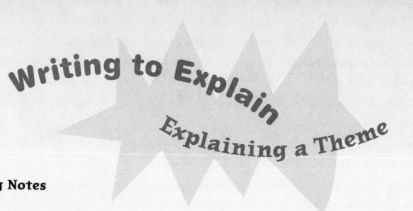

Writing to Explain
Explaining a Theme

Prewriting Notes

Below, write a theme you see in "Ali Baba." Choose one you talked about in class or one you thought of on your own.

A theme in "Ali Baba": _____

_____

_____

> Many parts, or **elements**, make up a great story. You have learned about a number of story elements: character, plot, and setting. You have also learned about theme. Writing about the other elements can help you explain a theme you see in the story.

Circle one or two other story elements you will write about to help you explain the theme you chose:

Character   **Plot**   **Setting**

Story element 1: _____

How it helps you explain the theme:

_____

_____

_____

_____

_____

Continue ⟶

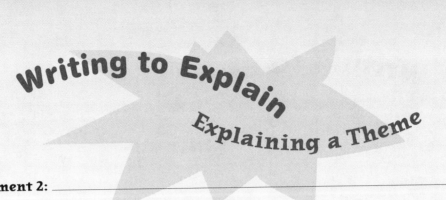

Writing to Explain
Explaining a Theme

Story element 2: _____

How it helps you explain the theme:

_____

_____

_____

_____

_____

_____

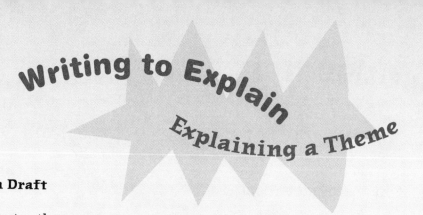

Writing to Explain
Explaining a Theme

Writing a Draft

Write about a theme you see in "Ali Baba and the Forty Thieves." Show how the story elements you chose help you explain this theme. Remember to use evidence from the story.

_____

_____

_____

_____

_____

_____

_____

_____

_____

_____

_____

_____

_____

_____

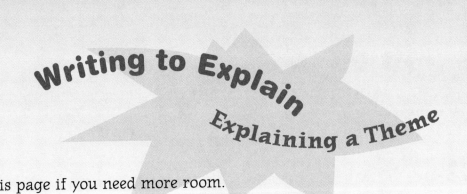

Writing to Explain

Explaining a Theme

Use this page if you need more room.

_____

_____

_____

_____

_____

_____

_____

_____

_____

_____

_____

_____

_____

_____

_____

_____

_____

Writing to Explore
Finding Treasure

Prewriting Notes

Imagine that, like Ali Baba, you find a cave full of treasure. What would you do? Would you take anything, and if so, what would it be? Think about these things before writing some notes in the first column of the chart on the next page.

Next, imagine that someone discovers you in the cave. Who finds you? What would you do? How would you feel? Would you go back to the cave? Think about these things and write some notes about the middle and end of your story in the chart on the next page.

Writing to Explore
Finding Treasure

Beginning: A description of the cave you find, and what you do when you find it

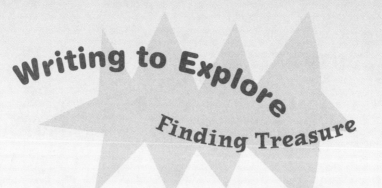

Writing to Explore
Finding Treasure

Middle: How you are discovered, and what happens	**End:** What happens after you are discovered, and how you feel because of what happened

Writing a Draft

Using your prewriting notes, draft your story about finding treasure in the space below. Make sure your story has a beginning, a middle, and an end, and include as much detail as possible.

Writing to Explore
Finding Treasure

Use this page if you need more room.

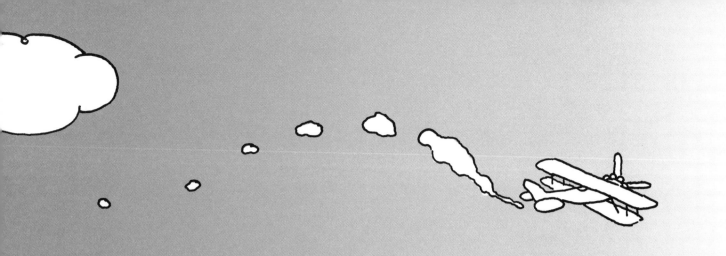

Writing Notebook

This is your chance to look back at what you have written in your Reader's Journal, choose a piece you wrote that you like, and make it the best it can be. Here's how to revise your draft:

1. Choose the Writing to Explain piece you wrote that you would most like to revise.

2. Mark the page with a paper clip or a sticky note and turn in your Reader's Journal to your teacher. Your teacher will write a question or note on the planning page (page 144, 148, or 152) for you to think about.

3. Read and think about your teacher's note. Review the story and your Reader's Journal for more ideas.

4. Plan your revised writing in the prewriting notes section (page 145, 149, or 153). Then write your revised draft on the next page.

Writing Notebook
Planning Page

Choose a piece to revise about one of these stories (circle one):

Shrewd Todie and Lyzer the Miser   **The Goldfish**   **The Great Blackberry Pick**

It is on page _____ of the Reader's Journal.

Think about your teacher's note to help you make your writing shine.

_____ **Write more details about character traits.**

Teacher's note: _____

_____

_____

_____ **Give more evidence about how the setting affects a character.**

Teacher's note: _____

_____

_____

_____ **Explain the problems and solutions more clearly.**

Teacher's note: _____

_____

_____

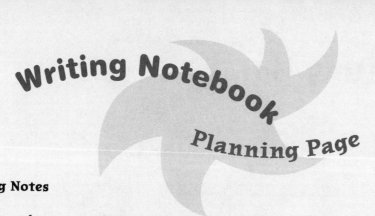

Writing Notebook
Planning Page

Prewriting Notes

Use a web, a chart, or a list to plan your writing.

Writing Notebook
Final Draft

Writing Notebook

Final Draft

Use this page if you need more room.

_____

_____

_____

_____

_____

_____

_____

_____

_____

_____

_____

_____

_____

_____

_____

_____

Writing Notebook
Planning Page

Choose a piece to revise about one of these stories (circle one):

The Story of Wang Li   The Hemulen Who Loved Silence   The Enchanted Sticks

It is on page _____ of the Reader's Journal.

Think about your teacher's note to help you make your writing shine.

_____ **Add or change details to make your explanation of a proverb clearer.**

Teacher's note: _____

_____

_____

_____ **Give more evidence about how the setting affects a character.**

Teacher's note: _____

_____

_____

_____ **Be more clear about the sequence of events in the story.**

Teacher's note: _____

_____

_____

Writing Notebook
Planning Page

Prewriting Notes

Use a web, chart, or list to plan your writing.

Writing Notebook

Final Draft

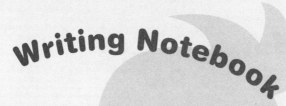

Writing Notebook

Final Draft

Use this page if you need more room.

_____

_____

_____

_____

_____

_____

_____

_____

_____

_____

_____

_____

_____

_____

_____

_____

_____

_____

Writing Notebook
Planning Page

Choose a piece to revise about one of these stories (circle one):

The Elephant's Child   **Mr. Singer's Nicknames**

The Little Humpbacked Horse   **Ali Baba and the Forty Thieves**

It is on page _____ of the Reader's Journal.

Think about your teacher's note to help you make your writing shine.

_____ **Describe the plot more clearly in your story summary.**

Teacher's note: _____

_____

_____

_____ **Explain more about a theme you see in the story.**

Teacher's note: _____

_____

_____

_____ **Write more about an element from the story such as setting, plot, or character.**

Teacher's note: _____

_____

_____

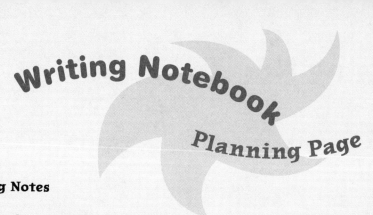

Writing Notebook
Planning Page

Prewriting Notes

Use a web, chart, or list to plan your writing.

Writing Notebook

Final Draft

_____

_____

_____

_____

_____

_____

_____

_____

_____

_____

_____

_____

_____

_____

_____

_____

_____

_____

_____

Writing Notebook

Final Draft

Use this page if you need more room.

_____

_____

_____

_____

_____

_____

_____

_____

_____

_____

_____

_____

_____

_____

_____

_____

_____

_____

_____

Curious Words

For each story, write down a curious word and the page number where the word appears. Then do one of the following:

• Write why you like your curious word, why it seems curious to you, or why you remember it.

• Pretend that one of the characters in the story uses your curious word and write down something the character says.

• Use your curious word in a message—for example, in a birthday or friendship card, in a poem, or in a funny note to a friend.

• Make up a fun way to use the word yourself.

Curious Words

Shrewd Todie and Lyzer the Miser

Your curious word _____ **page** _____

_____

_____

_____

Your curious word _____ **page** _____

_____

_____

_____

Your curious word _____ **page** _____

_____

_____

_____

Curious Words

The Goldfish

Your curious word _____ **page** _____

_____

_____

_____

_____

Your curious word _____ **page** _____

_____

_____

_____

_____

_____

Your curious word _____ **page** _____

_____

_____

_____

_____

Curious Words

The Great Blackberry Pick

Your curious word _____ page _____

_____

_____

_____

_____

Your curious word _____ page _____

_____

_____

_____

_____

Your curious word _____ page _____

_____

_____

_____

_____

Curious Words

The Story of Wang Li

Your curious word _____ **page** _____

_____

_____

_____

_____

Your curious word _____ **page** _____

_____

_____

_____

_____

Your curious word _____ **page** _____

_____

_____

_____

_____

Curious Words

The Hemulen Who Loved Silence

Your curious word _____ **page** _____

_____

_____

_____

_____

Your curious word _____ **page** _____

_____

_____

_____

_____

Your curious word _____ **page** _____

_____

_____

_____

_____

Curious Words

The Enchanted Sticks

Your curious word _____ **page** _____

_____

_____

_____

Your curious word _____ **page** _____

_____

_____

_____

Your curious word _____ **page** _____

_____

_____

_____

Curious Words

The Elephant's Child

Your curious word _____ page _____

_____

_____

_____

Your curious word _____ page _____

_____

_____

_____

Your curious word _____ page _____

_____

_____

_____

Curious Words

Mr. Singer's Nicknames

Your curious word _____ **page** _____

_____

_____

_____

_____

Your curious word _____ **page** _____

_____

_____

_____

_____

Your curious word _____ **page** _____

_____

_____

_____

_____

Curious Words

The Little Humpbacked Horse

Your curious word _____ page _____

_____

_____

_____

_____

Your curious word _____ page _____

_____

_____

_____

_____

Your curious word _____ page _____

_____

_____

_____

_____

Curious Words

Ali Baba and the Forty Thieves

Your curious word _____ **page** _____

_____

_____

_____

_____

Your curious word _____ **page** _____

_____

_____

_____

_____

Your curious word _____ **page** _____

_____

_____

_____

Glossary

In this glossary, you'll find definitions for words you may not know, but that are in the stories you've read. You'll find the meaning of each word as it is used in the story. The word may have other meanings as well, which you can find in a dictionary if you're interested. If you don't find a word here that you're wondering about, go to your dictionary for help.

abated: To **abate** is to become less intense or to die down. The woman's anger **abated** when she saw that the puppy was chewing on a bone, not her favorite shoes.

accommodation: A place to stay or sleep.

accomplices: An **accomplice** is someone who helps another person do something wrong or illegal. The two men supplied the bank robber with weapons, so the police considered them **accomplices**.

accustomed: When you are **accustomed** to something, you are used to it. If you go to bed every night at nine-thirty, you will become **accustomed** to going to sleep at that time.

acknowledge: When you **acknowledge** something, you admit that it exists or is true. If you have just gotten ready to go outside to play, you might not want to **acknowledge** that it has started to rain. The pain in his shoulder might get better if he would **acknowledge** the problem and go to the doctor.

admonished: When you **admonish** someone, you scold the person in a kind but serious way. "Don't wander off again—I was so worried," the girl's mother **admonished**.

afforestation: A man-made forest of trees. The **afforestation** of pine trees was planted in straight rows to make them easier to cut down.

agitated: When someone is **agitated**, he or she is very upset, nervous, or worried. The girl was **agitated** because it was raining and she was carrying a science project that couldn't get wet.

ajar: If something is **ajar**, that means it is partly open. If you leave the door **ajar** in the summer, mosquitoes can get in the house.

alighted: When you **alight** from something (such as a horse), you get off of it or down from it. The girl **alighted** from the swings when her turn was over.

Allah: Arabic for *God* or *the Supreme Being*.

amiable: Friendly and pleasant. The **amiable** bus driver always smiles and says hello when we get on the bus.

anemones: Sea **anemones** are colorful animals that live in the ocean and are shaped like tubes, with feelers around their mouths, making them look like flowers.

anoraks: Heavy hooded jackets. **Anoraks** are usually waterproof and very warm.

apprenticeship: A period of time spent working for someone without pay while learning that person's trade or skill. The young merchant spent his **apprenticeship** working in his aunt's shop, learning the business, and preparing to open his own shop.

ascertain: When you **ascertain** something, you find it out or figure it out. If you are going to bring cookies for your class, you need to **ascertain** whether you have enough for everyone.

assented: To **assent** means to agree to something. I thanked my mother when she **assented** to drive me to the mall.

august: An **august** person is someone grand and noble, worthy of respect. The **august** judge had many years of experience and was known for being fair. For this meaning, **august** is pronounced au-gúst.

avarice: A strong desire for wealth that cannot be satisfied; greediness.

awl: A pointed tool used for making small holes in leather or wood.

awry: When something has gone **awry**, that means it has gone wrong or off-course. The party went **awry** because the guest of honor was three hours late.

bade: If you **bade** someone hello or goodbye, you said it to them. **Bade** is the past tense of *bid*.

barrel organ: A large music box that plays a song when you turn the handle.

battens: A **batten** is a thin strip of wood.

becalmed: A sailing ship is **becalmed** when it is not moving because there is no wind to fill the sails.

benevolence: Kindness and goodwill toward others. The man was known for his **benevolence**—he gave almost all his money to the poor. My neighbor showed her **benevolence** by letting me play in her yard even after I rode my bike through her flower bed.

bestowed: To **bestow on** or **bestow upon** means to give something—usually a gift or a prize. Your teacher might **bestow** presents **on** the class for good attendance.

bitterly: When you do something **bitterly**, you do it with a deep, long-lasting anger or with deep disappointment. You might think **bitterly** about a game of tennis that you lost to someone who cheated.

bluebottles: Large, shiny blue-black flies.

bodes: To **bode** is to be a sign of something to come, either good or bad. That horse has won five other races this season, which **bodes** well for him in this race.

borscht: A kind of soup made with beets and other vegetables.

boyars: Russian noblemen.

bramble: A bush or shrub with thorns on the stems. Blackberry and raspberry bushes are two different types of **brambles**.

brittle: When something is **brittle**, it can break or snap easily. The dry, **brittle** leaves crunched under our feet as we ran through the yard.

brocade: A heavy cloth woven with a raised design.

bungalow: A small house, usually with only one floor.

burrowing: To **burrow** is to make a hole or a tunnel through something. The arctic fox went **burrowing** into the snow to keep warm.

capers, capering: A **caper** is a playful jump or leap. The puppy was doing **capers** around my feet, wanting me to throw the ball. If you are **capering**, you are jumping around happily and playfully.

caravan: A large group of people traveling together. A **caravan** can also contain vehicles and pack animals, like horses, donkeys, or camels.

caress: To **caress** something means to touch or stroke it gently. You might **caress** the soft fur of a kitten.

carrion: Dead, rotting flesh.

ceremoniously: When you do something **ceremoniously**, you do it in a formal, serious way, following the rules. At the end of the wedding, the minister **ceremoniously** announced, "I now pronounce you husband and wife."

chartreuse: A bright yellow-green color.

circumnavigation: Going completely around something. The explorer's goal was **circumnavigation** of the earth.

circumstances: The conditions that affect an event or a place are its **circumstances**. It's 70 degrees outside and sunny; under those **circumstances**, we won't be going sledding.

cleaned: When you **clean** a fish, you remove its insides, such as the stomach and intestines.

cobbler: Someone who makes and fixes shoes for a living.

compassion: A deep understanding of the suffering of others, along with the desire to ease that suffering. The children felt such **compassion** for the baby bird they found that they took it inside and made it a nest in a shoebox. When I hurt my leg and had to use crutches, my friend showed her **compassion** by always slowing down to walk with me.

comply, complied: When you **comply** with a rule or a request, you follow it or do what is asked. The boy **complied** with his father's request to stay inside during the hailstorm.

composed: When you **compose** yourself, you make yourself quiet and calm. The girl jumped when she heard a noise behind her, but she **composed** herself after realizing it was only a cat.

conferred: When you **confer** with someone, you meet with that person to discuss something. My brother and I **conferred** about how to get the kitchen chairs up to our tree house.

conscience, consciences: Your **conscience** is the feeling you have about what is right and what is wrong. Our **consciences** tell us that stealing and lying are wrong. You could not, in good **conscience**, pretend to be sick to stay home from school.

considerable: Fairly large in size or amount. There was a **considerable** crowd of people at the concert, so they had to add extra seats. It would cost a **considerable** amount of money to buy a treat for everyone in my school.

conspicuous: When something is **conspicuous**, it stands out; it is easy for people to notice. If you are very shy, you might think speaking in class makes you too **conspicuous**. The girl's pen leaked, leaving a **conspicuous** ink stain on her shirt.

conviction: A strongly held belief. We're going hiking this summer because my mother holds the **conviction** that we should get more fresh air and exercise.

counsel: Advice or a plan about what to do. Your best friend might give you **counsel** about what shirt to wear for school pictures.

courtiers: A **courtier** is a person who waits on a king or queen.

crestfallen: When you are **crestfallen**, you are feeling down or depressed about something. **Crestfallen** over the loss of the game, the team went out for ice cream to cheer themselves up.

cunning: A person who is **cunning** is good at tricking or fooling people. It takes great **cunning** to fool my mother–she always knows when I'm up to something. Because he was full of **cunning**, the farmer was able to make everyone believe that his sheep had magic wool.

cunningly: Cleverly; with skill. The old magician performed all his card tricks so **cunningly**, we couldn't figure out how he'd done them.

currying: To **curry** a horse is to comb and brush its coat.

cutlass: A heavy sword with a wide, flat, curved blade.

cutlery: Knives, forks, and spoons.

damped: When something has been **damped**, it has been weakened. The sad news **damped** our spirits.

deign: When you **deign** to do something, you do it even though you think you are too good for such things. The queen would not **deign** to speak with the townspeople. **Deign** rhymes with *rain*.

dejectedly: In a very sad way; with low spirits. After looking for her missing dog for two hours without finding it, the girl walked **dejectedly** home.

deprivation: People feel **deprivation** when they don't have things they need, such as shelter, clothing, and food. The Pilgrims faced great **deprivation** when they arrived in North America until the Wampanoag tribe helped them find food.

desolate: A place that is **desolate** does not have people living there. If your family were to move, your old home would be **desolate** until someone else moved in.

despair: Complete loss of hope. The woman was in **despair** after her wallet was stolen.

despicable: When something is **despicable**, it is hateful and people look down on it. Many Americans in the nineteenth century fought to end the **despicable** practice of slavery.

deterred, deterrent: When you are **deterred** from doing something, you have been stopped from doing it. A **deterrent** keeps something from happening. Bug spray is a **deterrent** against mosquito bites.

dire: Something **dire** is desperate. If you are very, very thirsty, you are in **dire** need of water.

disclose: When you **disclose** something, you make it known. This afternoon, the principal will **disclose** who won the costume contest.

discreet: If you are **discreet**, you are thoughtful about how you behave, especially about what to say and what to keep to yourself. Spies must be **discreet** so that no one finds out who they really are.

disperse, dispersed: To **disperse** is to scatter or to move apart in different directions. After a bat eats fruit, it will **disperse** the seeds far and wide while it flies. At the end of the play, the crowd slowly **dispersed** until the theater was empty.

disquieted: When you are **disquieted**, you are troubled, worried, or uneasy. After watching the scary movie, the boy was too **disquieted** to fall asleep.

diverged: To **diverge** is to go in a different direction or to leave the planned route. The runner got lost after he accidentally **diverged** from the rest of the group at a fork in the road.

divulge: When you **divulge** something, you are giving information that is supposed to be secret or private. I wouldn't **divulge** the location of our secret club to my little brother.

dolt: A stupid person. She said, "Everyone knows the earth is round, you **dolt**!"

dowry: Money or property that a woman brings to a marriage.

dread: When you feel **dread**, you feel uneasy because you think something unpleasant might happen. My brother has a strong **dread** of thunderstorms.

dreadful: Very bad or awful. You might think another student's behavior is **dreadful** if he hurts people's feelings or doesn't listen to the teacher.

dreary: When something is **dreary**, it is boring and a little gloomy. Cleaning your room can be a **dreary** task, especially if there are other things you'd rather be doing.

dullard: A person who is considered stupid.

dulled: To **dull** something is to make it less bright or clear. A fog hung over the city and **dulled** the light. Watching television for five hours in a row **dulled** his mind.

duly: Happening at the expected time, or just like it is supposed to. At a store, when you pay for something, the cashier takes your money and **duly** gives you a receipt.

dunderhead: A stupid person.

dupe: A person who is easy to trick or fool. My little sister is a **dupe**—I once convinced her that our dog had said my name.

elaborate: With great care and attention to detail. The **elaborate** carving was done so well, the flowers and leaves looked almost real.

elapsed: When something **elapses**, it goes by or passes. Five years **elapsed** before he saw his cousin again.

endurance: The ability to keep going for a long time. People have tried to set **endurance** records for things like standing on one foot or dancing without stopping.

enticing: When something is **enticing**, it is appealing and you want it. The cookies in the bakery window were so **enticing** that they made my mouth water.

envious: When you are **envious**, you feel uncomfortable because you want something that someone else has. I am not envious of my friend for his new lunch box, because I like to carry my lunch in a paper bag.

equerry: An officer in charge of the horses in a royal or noble household.

erred: When you **err**, you make a mistake or an **error**. In 1492, Christopher Columbus **erred** in thinking he had reached Asia (he was actually in America). To **err** is also to commit a wrongdoing. I **erred** in taking my friend's homework and turning it in as my own.

esteem: If you have **esteem** for someone, you respect and admire that person.

eventually: After a while, or in the end. We waited and waited, but **eventually** we had to go to the movies without her.

exception: Something that is not included in the general rule or situation. Everyone in my family has brown eyes, with the **exception** of my little brother, who has blue eyes.

exile: A person who is sent away from his or her country or home and not allowed to come back.

extinguished: When you **extinguish** something (such as a flame or a light), you put it out. The woman **extinguished** the candle before going to bed.

fate: The force that some people believe decides what happens in life and how things will turn out. I think it is my **fate** to become a writer when I get older. She believes it was **fate** that brought her to work here.

fidgeting: When you **fidget**, you move around in an uneasy or nervous way. You might start **fidgeting** if the principal called you to her office and you had to wait outside.

filial: Acting in a way that is proper for a son or daughter. The **filial** daughter always gave her mother flowers for her birthday.

flinched: When you **flinch**, you make a quick movement away from something that is painful, dangerous, or unpleasant. I **flinched** when the doctor gave me a shot.

floundered: To **flounder** is to move clumsily or stumble about. I **floundered** on the icy driveway, slipping and sliding as I tried to keep my balance.

flourish: To **flourish** is to grow well and become strong. Plants will **flourish** if you give them the sunlight and water they need.

forfeit, forfeited: As a noun, a **forfeit** is something you give up or surrender as punishment for a crime, an accident, or a mistake. The **forfeit** for littering in the park is fifty dollars. As a verb, to **forfeit** means to lose something or to have to give it up. The team **forfeited** the game because only two of their players showed up.

fraud: The act of tricking or cheating people.

frenzy: A state of wild excitement. The boy ran around the room in a **frenzy** when he got his new bike. The cook was in a **frenzy** trying to finish cooking a meal for one hundred people by herself.

frisked: To **frisk** is to play in a lively way. The lion cubs **frisked** around their mother, playfully trying to bite one another.

gaudy: Bright and a little too flashy. My aunt's **gaudy** shoes were covered with fake diamonds and pink glitter.

gaze: To look at something steadily, with fixed attention—especially something unusually beautiful or amazing. You might **gaze** at a rainbow or at a whale swimming, but not at a sidewalk or a school bus.

gewgaws: Small, useless items or knickknacks. My grandma has a collection of glass figures and other **gewgaws**.

glint: A brief flash or sparkle of light. I saw a **glint** through the window as the car pulled into the driveway.

gongs: A **gong** is a piece of metal shaped like a plate that is used as a musical instrument. **Gongs** make deep sounds when you play them by striking them with a hammer.

gratitude: A feeling of being thankful. The family felt deep **gratitude** toward the firefighter who rescued them. If your parents were to fix you your favorite meal, you might show your **gratitude** by washing the dishes afterward.

grieves, grieving: To **grieve** is to feel great sadness. It always **grieves** me to hear news of a fire or accident.

hastily: When you do something **hastily**, you do it too quickly or you haven't really thought it through. If you left your house **hastily**, you might forget your lunch or your book bag.

haunches: The upper thigh, hip, and backside area of an animal. When a dog rests, it sits on its **haunches**.

hinder: To hold back, get in the way, or make it difficult to do something. A crowd of people standing in the doorway might **hinder** you from entering a room.

hips: The **hip** is the part of a rose that holds the seeds.

hoisted: You **hoist** something when you lift or pull it up. The tall crane **hoisted** heavy pieces of metal and wood into the air.

hospitably: When you treat visitors or guests **hospitably**, you treat them in a friendly and welcoming way. The server at our favorite restaurant always greets us with a smile and treats us **hospitably**.

hue and cry: A noisy public demand or protest. The neighbors raised a **hue and cry** about the air pollution from the factory in their town.

imam: The person who leads prayer at a *mosque* (a Muslim temple).

impenetrable: Impossible to get through or past. We looked around for a door or an opening, but the wall was **impenetrable**.

implore: To beg strongly. I **implore** you not to jump into the pool if you don't know how to swim.

impudently: Something that happens **impudently** happens in a rude, bold way. The door slammed **impudently** in my face.

incense: A substance that is burned to give off a pleasant smell. **Incense** usually comes in the form of long, thin sticks or small cones.

incomparable: When something is **incomparable**, it is so excellent that there is nothing else like it. Prizewinning racehorses can run with **incomparable** swiftness. My grandmother's oatmeal cookies are **incomparable**—nobody else's are as good.

incurring: To **incur** something is to become responsible for it, or to bring it on yourself. When you get a pet, you are **incurring** the tasks of feeding and caring for it.

indignant, indignantly: If you are **indignant**, you are upset and angry because you feel that something is not fair. You might stomp off to your room **indignantly** if your parents punished you for something you did not do. If your sister is making fun of your new haircut, you might **indignantly** tell her to stop.

ingenuity: Cleverness and imagination. She showed **ingenuity** in making a desk out of concrete blocks with a board across the top. Alexander Graham Bell's **ingenuity** led him to invent the telephone.

ingots: Pieces of metal (usually gold or silver) that have been shaped into blocks or bars.

inquisitive: Curious or eager to learn. The **inquisitive** dog explored the backyard, sniffing and poking its nose into the bushes and piles of leaves. An **inquisitive** student asks the teacher lots of questions about the subject being studied.

insatiable: See **'satiable**.

insurance representative: Someone in charge of handling business for an **insurance** company. You can buy **insurance** so that the **insurance** company will then pay you in case of sickness, fire, accident, or theft.

intention: Something you plan or mean to do. I had the **intention** of buying some milk for my mom, but the store was closed. It might be your **intention** to read a new book each week over the summer.

issuing forth: To **issue forth** is to come out of something. A stream of water was **issuing forth** from the broken fire hydrant.

jade: A hard green stone used for making ornaments, sculptures, and jewelry. **Jade** is very important in Chinese history and culture.

keen: Sharp or quick in seeing, hearing, or thinking. Dogs have a **keen** sense of smell and are able to smell things that humans can't.

kimonos: A **kimono** is a traditional Japanese robe with wide sleeves and a wide belt.

kindling: Small, thin pieces of wood used for starting a fire.

lacquer: A substance that is put on a surface and dries to a very shiny coat. **Lacquer** is used on some types of furniture as well as plates and bowls.

lament: A display of great sadness. The singer's **lament** for her lost love brought tears to our eyes.

larder: A small room or closet where food is stored.

lavish: Describes something when it is more than is needed or grand and expensive. My great-uncle is known for throwing **lavish** parties with fancy food and decorations.

limpid: Perfectly clear. We could see all the way to the bottom of the **limpid** pond.

livelihood: Your **livelihood** is the way that you make money to support yourself or earn a living. Taking care of a garden can be either a hobby or a **livelihood**.

locust: A **locust** is a kind of grasshopper. **Locusts** travel in large swarms and eat crops.

makeshift: Something that is used as a replacement for something else, using things that are already on hand. The girls put a sheet over the tops of two chairs to create a **makeshift** fort.

malice: A feeling of wanting to hurt someone or see them in pain. It takes great **malice** to get a classmate in trouble with the principal by telling lies about him.

marrow: The soft material that fills the hollow parts of bones. **Marrow** is used by your body to make red and white blood cells.

meditated: To **meditate** is to train or calm your mind, typically by focusing on something. The woman **meditated** every morning by paying attention to her breathing while she walked through the park.

menacingly: Something that is **menacing** is threatening or dangerous. **Menacing** storm clouds made the teacher decide to move the class picnic into the gym.

meshes: The open spaces in a net, or the cords or threads surrounding these spaces. Sometimes leaves get caught in the **meshes** of the net used to clean the swimming pool.

mime: If you **mime** something, you act it out using your hands and body movements, without speaking. I couldn't hear my mother through the window, but I saw her **mime** that it was time to come inside for dinner.

miscellaneous: Something that is **miscellaneous** is made up of different things or parts. Sock drawers usually contain some **miscellaneous** unmatched socks. I have a box under my bed where I keep my **miscellaneous** things—beads, buttons, key chains, marbles, rocks, and shells.

miser: A **miser** is a person who does not want to spend or share his or her money. My brother is such a **miser** that he would rather eat my leftover ice cream than spend his money to buy his own.

mock: Something that is **mock** is an imitation or not real. Her **mock** diamond earrings weren't as expensive as real ones.

mosque: A Muslim house of worship.

mournful: Showing or feeling great sadness. The **mournful** child cried for hours after she lost her balloon.

mulberry: A **mulberry** is a sweet, black fruit that grows on a tree. Silkworms eat the leaves of certain **mulberry** trees.

murmur, murmured: As a noun, a **murmur** is a low, steady sound that is not very clear. As a verb, to **murmur** something is to say it in a quiet voice. The shy student **murmured** an answer that her teacher could barely hear.

musky: A **musky** smell is a very strong smell that usually comes from a male animal. You might notice a **musky** odor when you visit the deer cage at the zoo.

nappies: British word for *diapers*.

no avail: Something that is of **no avail** has no use or benefit. Your trip to the library would be of **no avail** if the book you need has already been checked out.

nonplussed: If you are **nonplussed**, you are so confused or puzzled that you don't know what to say or do. After my parents announced we were moving to another state, my brother and I were so **nonplussed** that we all just stood there in silence.

obliging: An **obliging** person is ready to do favors or to help out. My **obliging** classmate loaned me a pencil after I forgot mine again. In turn, I felt very **obliging** when she asked to borrow lunch money.

obstinate: Stubborn and unwilling to change one's mind. My **obstinate** little brother refused to go to bed even though it was after midnight and he was exhausted.

ordains: If you **ordain** something, you have the authority or legal power to require it. The law **ordains** that all young people must attend school.

overwhelming: If something is **overwhelming** it floods over you in a powerful way. The bright sunshine was so **overwhelming** that it stung my eyes.

pachyderm: The scientific name for thick-skinned animals with hooves. Elephants, rhinoceros, and hippopotamuses are all **pachyderms**.

pagoda: A tower with a roof that curves upward on each story. **Pagodas** are usually found in Asian countries.

parry: To avoid a blow or block it by pushing it away. You might try to **parry** a water balloon thrown at you.

parsonage: A **parsonage** is the official home given by a church to its pastor.

partook: The past tense of *partake*, which means to take part in or participate in something. The girl **partook** in every single ride at the carnival.

Passover: A Jewish holiday lasting eight days in the spring to remember the escape of the Jews from slavery in Egypt.

pattered: To **patter** is to make light, quick sounds. The rain **pattered** gently on the roof.

pavilions: Open-sided structures used for shelter or entertainment.

pendulum: A weight that is hung in such a way that it can swing back and forth. The tick-tock noise you hear in a grandfather clock is the **pendulum** swinging back and forth.

pension: Money that is paid to someone after he or she has retired. After many years of hard work, my grandfather now lives on his monthly **pension**.

perceiving: To **perceive** something is to become aware of it through your senses, such as sight or hearing. An owl is good at **perceiving** any kind of movement when it's dark outside. I have an easy time **perceiving** my friend's moods—she always hums when she's happy, and she gets very quiet when she's angry.

permanently: Forever. The store went out of business and shut its doors **permanently**.

perpetrated: To **perpetrate** is to be responsible for doing something, usually something bad. The man who **perpetrated** the crime went to prison for many years.

perplexed: Confused or puzzled. You might be **perplexed** if your older sister suddenly started being extra-nice to you when she had always ignored you before. After losing the instructions, he was **perplexed** about how to put together the model airplane.

pince-nez: Eyeglasses that clip to the nose.

pips: Small seeds of a fruit.

plaster: British word for *bandage*.

pledge: A sincere promise. The student made a **pledge** never again to cheat.

pondered: You **ponder** when you think carefully about something. You might **ponder** whether you really want to join an after-school club.

poods: A **pood** is a weight measurement equal to thirty-six pounds. Twelve **poods** is equal to 432 pounds.

port: The left side of a ship.

precautions: A **precaution** is something you do in order to prevent harm or danger. When we go camping, we take along a first aid kit and extra matches as **precautions**.

precisely: Exactly. My grandmother always gives me **precisely** what I want for my birthday because she knows me so well. The train to the city leaves the station at **precisely** 9:07.

predecessor: A **predecessor** is the person who held a job or position before another person. The new coach wasn't well liked at first because his **predecessor** had been so popular with the team.

profound: If something is **profound**, it comes from deep inside you. I have a **profound** fear of mice, but spiders don't bother me at all.

prowess: Outstanding or excellent skill or ability. The cat showed **prowess** when it jumped from the balcony to the tree branch to chase the squirrel.

punctually: To do something **punctually** is to do it on time. It is always best to show up **punctually** to any appointment or date.

queer: Odd or unusual. A snowy day would be a **queer** time to have a picnic.

quip: A witty or clever remark. My friend always has a clever **quip** on the tip of his tongue. If you make your classmates laugh with your jokes and **quips**, they might call you the "class clown."

quivered: To **quiver** is to quickly shake or shiver just a little bit. My stomach **quivered** at the thought of riding the Ferris wheel.

rabbi: A leader and teacher of the Jewish religion.

radiating: If something is **radiating**, it is sending out waves or rays. Warmth and light were **radiating** from the campfire.

rash: If you are **rash**, you act quickly and without thinking first. My older brother made the **rash** decision to quit his job after he disagreed with his boss. It would be **rash** of you to do something dangerous just because someone dared you.

receded: To **recede** is to move back or fade away. My father's hairline **receded** a little more each year until he was completely bald. The ocean **receded** at low tide and left seashells on the sand.

refrained: To **refrain** is to keep yourself from doing something. I **refrained** from chewing gum in class, although I really wanted a piece.

regale: In this case, to **regale** is to eat a feast or to eat a lot.

reluctantly: If you do something **reluctantly**, you don't really want to do it. I washed the dishes **reluctantly** because I wanted to play outside instead.

repented: To **repent** is to feel deeply sorry for doing something. The boy **repented** yelling at his friend.

reproached: To **reproach** is to blame someone or to express disapproval. My mother **reproached** me for walking through the house with wet shoes.

repute: To have **repute** is to have fame or a reputation. That restaurant has poor **repute**—people say it's dirty and the food is terrible.

requisite: Something that is **requisite** is required or necessary. Before we went to summer camp, our parents had to mail in the **requisite** forms.

retorted: To **retort** is to answer someone quickly or sharply. When the boy complained about his burnt toast, his sister **retorted** that he should make his own.

rind: The hard outer layer or skin on melons, citrus fruits, and some cheeses.

rites: A **rite** is a special action or ceremony.

roubles: A **rouble**, or *ruble*, is the main unit of money in Russia.

row: A noisy argument or fight. My two brothers got into an awful **row** and shouted at each other all night. In this case, **row** rhymes with *cow*.

rummage: To **rummage** is to look for something by moving things around in an untidy or careless way. If you **rummage** through your closet looking for a missing shoe, you might leave things a real mess.

ruses: A **ruse** is a clever trick meant to fool or mislead someone. If your family throws a surprise party for your sister's birthday, a **ruse** would get her to the party without making her suspicious.

rusk: A piece of bread that has been baked until it is dry and crisp.

Sabbath: The day of the week used for worship. For Jews, the **Sabbath** begins at sundown on Friday and ends at sundown on Saturday. Sunday is the **Sabbath** for Christians.

saddlebow: The upper front part of a saddle.

sage: A very wise person.

samisen: A Japanese musical instrument with a long neck and three strings.

'satiable (insatiable): When someone is **insatiable**, it is impossible to satisfy that person's needs or wants. In "The Elephant's Child," the author shortens the word to **'satiable**. The boy's **insatiable** curiosity about space led him to buy a telescope and read books about the stars and planets. I have an **insatiable** love of peanut butter, and could eat it at every meal.

satisfaction: If you feel **satisfaction**, you feel content with something. If you study very hard for a test, you might feel **satisfaction** when it's finally over and you know you did well.

sauntered: If you **saunter**, you walk at an easy, relaxed pace. If I have nothing to do, I like to **saunter** through the park. The teacher was angry when his student **sauntered** into class five minutes late.

scalded: To **scald** is to burn with very hot liquid or steam. The woman was **scalded** with soup when she knocked the pot off the stove.

scornfully: With a strong feeling of dislike for something you think is bad or worthless. My grandmother spoke **scornfully** to the thief who tried to steal her purse on the train.

scoured: If you **scour** an area of land, you move over it swiftly. We **scoured** the trail in record time.

seething: Something **seething** is churning and foaming. Water on the stove starts **seething** when it comes to a boil.

seized: To **seize** something is to grab or capture it. He **seized** his umbrella before the wind could blow it away.

serene, serenity: Something **serene** is calm and peaceful. The lake was **serene** after the storm passed. **Serenity** is calmness and peacefulness. My idea of **serenity** is spending an afternoon reading in a hammock.

severance: The act of being broken apart or separated. My sister and I pulled the ends of the wishbone until its **severance** decided whose wish would be granted.

severely: Something done **severely** is done in a stern or demanding way. Your parents might speak to you **severely** if you interrupt an important conversation.

sheath: A holder for a knife or sword.

shrewd: Clever and crafty. My sister is good at chess, so I have to be quite **shrewd** to beat her.

shroud: A cloth in which a body is wrapped for burial.

simpleton: A person who doesn't have much common sense or intelligence. After my father locked the keys in the car for the seventh time, my mother called him a **simpleton**.

simultaneously: At the same time. The twins do everything together—they even speak **simultaneously**.

slight: A **slight** is something you do that hurts someone's pride or confidence; a mild insult. If you walked past your friend without speaking to her, she might think it was a **slight**.

snouts: A **snout** is the front part of an animal's head that sticks out, including its nose, mouth, and jaw. Pigs' **snouts** are shaped to help them sniff and poke in the dirt for food.

soothingly: If you do something **soothingly**, you do it in a way that puts someone at ease or calms them down. When I am frightened, it helps if my mother strokes my hair **soothingly**.

sowed: To **sow** a crop is to plant it. The gardener **sowed** cabbage, carrots, onions, and tomatoes.

spats: Leather or cloth covers that go over the ankles and tops of shoes. **Spats** are usually fastened by straps under the shoes and buttons on one side.

speculate: To **speculate** is to buy or sell something in the hopes of making money when there is also a risk of losing money.

spindly: When something is **spindly**, it is long and thin, and often weak. The newborn colt stood shakily on its **spindly** legs.

stammered: When you **stammer**, you speak in an unsure way, stopping often and repeating certain sounds or words without meaning to. The embarrassed girl **stammered** an excuse for being late.

stinginess: Not wanting to spend money or share things with others, even when you have plenty. If your brother won't give you any of his candy, you might accuse him of **stinginess**. Because of his **stinginess**, the wealthy man would sit in the dark rather than turn on a lamp and pay for the electricity.

strewn: Scattered or spread all over. Flowers were **strewn** down the path where the bride was walking.

strongbox: A safe for locking away money or valuable things.

sucklings: A **suckling** is a baby or young animal that is still being nursed.

surpass: To go beyond or do better than what has been done before. When the video game expert plays, he always tries to **surpass** his previous score. In a race, you might try hard to **surpass** the fastest person's time and set the new record.

surrender: To **surrender** is to give up or admit to losing. The game lasted so many hours that one of the teams finally **surrendered**. I **surrendered** after several minutes of the arm wrestling contest because my shoulder began to hurt.

suspicion: When you have a **suspicion**, you have a strong feeling about something without knowing for sure. I had a **suspicion** that a party was taking place when I saw several children enter the house with wrapped presents.

swagger: To walk in a bold, proud way. You might **swagger** across the field after your team wins a soccer match.

swallow: A small, fast bird with long, pointed wings and a forked tail.

sweetmeats: Sweet treats, such as candied fruits and sugar-covered nuts.

switchback: British word for *roller coaster*.

systematically: If you do something **systematically**, you do it in a step-by-step, organized way. My parents do the dishes **systematically**: my father always washes and my mother always dries. If you did your homework **systematically**, you might start with your most challenging subject and end with your favorite.

tattered: If something is **tattered**, it is old and torn. My sister refuses to throw out her **tattered** basketball jersey even though it's full of holes.

tempest: A fierce, powerful storm. The **tempest** caused awful flood and wind damage throughout the town.

terraces: A **terrace** is a paved outdoor space right next to a building. The **terraces** on our block overlook the local stream.

thatched: A **thatched** roof is made out of strong plant stalks such as straw or reeds.

thicket: An area with lots of shrubs or bushes growing close together. My legs got scratched when I took a shortcut through the **thicket** behind our house.

thither: A way of saying "there" or "in that direction."

threshed: To **thresh** is to separate the grain or seed from a plant by striking or beating it. Today, wheat is typically **threshed** in very large machines.

throng: A large group of people gathered closely together. The **throng** of kids on the playground was making a lot of noise. I took a side street to avoid the **throng** of shoppers on the main street.

tiller: The handle used to steer a boat.

timid, timidly: To be **timid** is to hesitate out of fear or doubt. If you are **timid**, you might not want to be the first one to climb the rope in gym class. To do something **timidly** is to do it in a shy or fearful way. You might say hello very **timidly** to a large group of strangers.

toppling: If something is **toppling**, it is falling over or being knocked over. If you stack books very high, they might eventually start **toppling** over.

treacle tart: A molasses-flavored pie.

trellis: A frame of crisscrossed strips of wood or metal that supports a growing plant. My neighbors have roses growing on a **trellis** that is fastened to the side of their house.

tribute: A **tribute** is something done or said to show thanks or respect. A **tribute** might be in the form of an award, a speech, a party, or a gift.

trod: Walked on, over, or along something. **Trod** is the past tense of **tread**. The boys left their bikes behind and **trod** home on the dusty path.

tsar: Russia was ruled by an emperor, called a **tsar**, until the early 1900s.

tusky: A **tusk** is a long, large, pointed tooth that sticks out of the mouths of some animals, like elephants, walruses, and wild boars. To be **tusky** means to have tusks.

ulster: A loose, long overcoat made of heavy material.

unaccustomed: If you are **unaccustomed** to something, you are not used to it. When school starts after summer break, some students are **unaccustomed** to waking up early.

unanimously: If something is decided **unanimously**, it means that everyone agrees on a decision. We would have decided **unanimously** to go to the park, except that one person didn't want to go.

undutiful: An **undutiful** person doesn't do what he knows he should.

unobtrusive: Not in the way, or not very noticeable. The music was so **unobtrusive** that we barely realized it was playing.

upholstery: The stuffing, springs, cushions, and cloth coverings that are used to make furniture.

vapor: Thin mist, steam, or smoke. An airplane flying overhead leaves a trail of **vapor** in the sky.

vast: Huge or wide. If you watch the Superbowl, you might be impressed by the **vast** crowd attending the game. When you look out of an airplane window or see a picture taken from a plane, you can see how **vast** the world really is.

venerable: Someone **venerable** is worthy of special respect due to age, knowledge, or position in society. My grandparents are **venerable** because they are much older and wiser than I.

versts: A **verst** is a measurement of distance in Russia equal to about two-thirds of a mile. A thousand **versts** is about 663 miles.

vicinity: The **vicinity** is the area surrounding a particular place. If you live in the **vicinity** of the playground, you live near it.

vicious: Something or someone **vicious** is mean and fierce and might try to hurt others. The **vicious** dog barked and growled before it attacked. The **vicious** bully picks fights every day and trips people in the hallway.

vitiate: To **vitiate** something is to make it worthless or to lessen its quality. Your brother could **vitiate** your fun at the movies by talking so much that you can't hear the dialogue.

white caps: Waves with white foam on top.

wholly: Completely or entirely. If you are **wholly** certain you want to go to camp, that means you absolutely want to go.

wont: If you are **wont** to do something, you are used to doing it. He was **wont** to go for long walks, as he'd done every day for years.

wooing: If you **woo** someone, you seek that person's affection or attention. A man might begin **wooing** a woman by writing poems to her or giving her flowers.

wroth: An old-fashioned word that means angry or furious.